Solidity for Web3 Developers

A Hands-on Guide to Design, Deploy, and Interact with Smart Contracts

Corbin Husman

Copyright © 2024 Corbin Husman

All rights reserved. No part of this book may be reproduced, stored in a retrieval system, or transmitted, in any form or by any means, electronic, mechanical, photocopying, recording, or otherwise, without the prior written permission of the author, except in the case of brief quotations embodied in critical reviews and certain other noncommercial uses permitted by copyright law.

Disclaimer

This book is for educational and informational purposes only. It is not intended as financial, legal, or investment advice. The author and publisher do not guarantee accuracy, completeness, or timeliness of the information and are not responsible for errors or omissions.

Cryptocurrency and blockchain investments are highly speculative and involve significant risk. The author and publisher are not liable for any losses or damages incurred.

The views expressed are those of the author and do not reflect the publisher's views. Specific product or company mentions do not constitute endorsements.

Readers should conduct their own research and consult qualified professionals before making financial or investment decisions related to blockchain technology or cryptocurrencies.

Table of contents

Preface..6
Chapter 1: Introduction to Web3..9
   1.1 What is Web3?.. 9
   1.2 Key Concepts of Web3... 12
   1.3 The Role of Smart Contracts in Web3... 16
   1.4 Why Solidity?.. 20
Chapter 2: Getting Started with Solidity..24
   2.1 Setting Up Your Development Environment............................... 24
       2.1.1 Installing Necessary Tools... 24
       2.1.2 Choosing an IDE..28
   2.2 Basic Syntax and Data Types...31
   2.3 Writing Your First Smart Contract.. 36
   2.4 Compiling and Deploying with Remix... 39
Chapter 3: Understanding the Ethereum Blockchain................... 43
   3.1 What is Ethereum?... 43
   3.2 Accounts, Transactions, and Gas... 46
   3.3 Ethereum Virtual Machine (EVM).. 49
   3.4 Exploring the Ethereum Network (Mainnet, Testnets)................ 52
Chapter 4: Core Solidity Concepts... 57
   4.1 Functions and Modifiers..57
   4.2 Variables and Data Structures.. 61
   4.3 Control Flow and Error Handling... 66
   4.4 Events and Logging.. 71
Chapter 5: Smart Contract Security..74
   5.1 Common Vulnerabilities.. 75
   5.2 Security Best Practices... 80
   5.3 Testing and Auditing Smart Contracts.. 84
Chapter 6: Advanced Solidity..90
   6.1 Contract Inheritance and Interfaces...90
   6.2 Libraries and Using External Code.. 95
   6.3 Working with Low-level Calls... 99
   6.4 Gas Optimization Techniques.. 103

Chapter 7: ERC-20 Tokens 107
- 7.1 Understanding the ERC-20 Standard 107
- 7.2 Creating Your Own Token 110
- 7.3 Token Functionality (Transfer, Approve, etc.) 114

Chapter 8: NFTs (Non-Fungible Tokens) 121
- 8.1 What are NFTs? 121
- 8.2 The ERC-721 Standard 124
- 8.3 Creating and Managing NFTs 127
- 8.4 NFT Use Cases 131

Chapter 9: Decentralized Autonomous Organizations (DAOs) 137
- 9.1 Understanding DAO Concepts 137
- 9.2 Building a Basic DAO 140
- 9.3 Governance and Voting Mechanisms 146
- 9.4 DAO Security Considerations 150

Chapter 10: Interacting with Other Blockchains 156
- 10.1 Cross-chain Communication 156
- 10.2 Web3 Libraries and APIs 159
- 10.3 Exploring Other EVM-Compatible Chains 164

Chapter 11: The Future of Solidity and Web3 169
- 11.1 Emerging Trends and Technologies 169
- 11.2 Solidity Development Roadmap 174
- 11.3 The Evolving Web3 Landscape 178

Conclusion 182

Preface

Blockchain technology has opened up a whole new frontier of possibilities. From cryptocurrencies like Bitcoin and Ethereum to decentralized finance (DeFi) and non-fungible tokens (NFTs), we're witnessing a paradigm shift in how we think about digital ownership, value, and interaction.

At the heart of this revolution are smart contracts – self-executing contracts with the terms of the agreement directly written into code. These Amazing pieces of software automate transactions, eliminate intermediaries, and create trustless systems where participants can interact directly with each other.

Solidity is the language that brings these smart contracts to life. It's a powerful tool that allows you to create decentralized applications that can revolutionize industries and empower users. This book was born out of a passion for Web3 and a desire to make Solidity accessible to everyone who wants to build the future of the internet.

This book aims to provide a practical and comprehensive guide to Solidity for Web3 developers. We'll start with the basics, covering the fundamentals of Web3, blockchain technology, and the Ethereum ecosystem. Then we'll explore the core concepts of Solidity, from syntax and data types to functions, control flow, and object-oriented programming.

We'll go beyond the basics, examining security best practices, advanced Solidity features, and popular smart contract patterns like ERC-20 tokens and NFTs. You'll learn how to design, deploy, and interact with smart contracts, and we'll even build some simple decentralized applications together.

While we'll cover a lot of ground, this book doesn't attempt to be an exhaustive encyclopedia of Solidity. Instead, it focuses on providing a solid foundation and practical skills that you can use to explore further and build your own amazing dApps.

This book is written for aspiring Web3 developers with some programming experience who are eager to learn Solidity and build decentralized applications. Whether you're a student, a hobbyist, or a professional developer looking to expand your skills, you'll find valuable insights and practical guidance within these pages.

No prior experience with blockchain or Solidity is required. We'll introduce the necessary concepts gradually, ensuring that everyone can follow along.

The book is divided into four parts:

- Part I: Foundations: We'll lay the groundwork by exploring the core concepts of Web3, blockchain technology, and the Ethereum ecosystem.
- Part II: Designing Smart Contracts: We'll learn the ins and outs of Solidity, from basic syntax to advanced features and security considerations.
- Part III: Building dApps: We'll put our Solidity skills to practice by building real-world decentralized applications, including tokens, NFTs, and DAOs.
- Part IV: Beyond Ethereum: We'll explore other blockchain platforms and the future of Solidity and Web3.

Each chapter builds upon the previous ones, providing a clear and logical progression. Code examples, exercises, and practical tips are sprinkled throughout to reinforce learning and encourage experimentation.

So, are you ready to embark on this exciting adventure into the world of Web3 and Solidity? Grab your favorite code editor, fire up your development environment, and let's build some amazing decentralized applications together! I hope you find this book informative, engaging, and inspiring. Happy coding!

Chapter 1: Introduction to Web3

Welcome to the exciting world of Web3! If you're curious about blockchain, decentralized applications (dApps), and the future of the internet, you've come to the right place. This chapter will introduce you to the key concepts of Web3 and set the stage for your journey into Solidity and smart contract development.

1.1 What is Web3?

Web3, on the other hand, is more like a bustling marketplace. You still have many different vendors (websites and applications), but there's no single entity in control. The marketplace operates on a shared infrastructure (blockchain technology), and the rules are governed by the community. You have more freedom to choose which vendors you interact with, and you have more control over your own data and digital assets.

Key Characteristics of Web3

Here are some defining characteristics of Web3:

- Decentralization: Web3 aims to distribute power and control away from centralized entities like big tech companies and governments. It leverages technologies like blockchain and peer-to-peer networks to create a more distributed and resilient internet. This means that there's no single point of failure or control, making it more resistant to censorship and outages.
- User Ownership: In Web3, users have more control over their data and digital identity. They can choose how their data is used and shared, and they can own and manage their digital assets without relying on intermediaries. It's like having your own personal vault where you store your valuables, and you decide who has access to them.

- Transparency: Web3 promotes transparency by using open-source technologies and decentralized platforms. Transactions and interactions are often recorded on public blockchains, making them auditable and verifiable by anyone. It's like having a public record of all transactions in the marketplace, ensuring accountability and preventing fraud.
- Security: Web3 leverages cryptographic techniques and blockchain technology to enhance security and prevent unauthorized access or tampering with data. It's like having a strong security system in place to protect your valuables and prevent theft or vandalism.
- Interoperability: Web3 aims to create a more interconnected and interoperable internet where different platforms and applications can communicate seamlessly. This allows for greater flexibility and innovation, as developers can build applications that work together without relying on proprietary APIs or centralized platforms. It's like having a universal language that everyone in the marketplace understands, facilitating trade and collaboration.

Examples of Web3 Applications

Here are some concrete examples of how Web3 is being used today:

- Cryptocurrencies: Bitcoin and Ethereum are examples of decentralized cryptocurrencies that operate on blockchain networks without central authorities. They allow for peer-to-peer transactions without the need for intermediaries like banks.
- Decentralized Finance (DeFi): DeFi applications provide financial services like lending, borrowing, and trading without intermediaries like banks. They use smart contracts

to automate transactions and create trustless financial systems.
- Non-Fungible Tokens (NFTs): NFTs represent unique digital assets, like artwork, collectibles, or virtual real estate, that are owned and managed by users on blockchain networks. They provide a way to establish ownership and provenance of digital assets, opening up new possibilities for creators and collectors.
- Decentralized Autonomous Organizations (DAOs): DAOs are organizations governed by code and run by communities, allowing for decentralized decision-making and governance. They use smart contracts to automate operations and ensure transparency and accountability.
- Decentralized Social Media: Web3 is enabling the creation of decentralized social media platforms where users have more control over their data and interactions. These platforms are often resistant to censorship and provide greater privacy and security.
- Supply Chain Management: Blockchain technology can be used to track goods and materials throughout the supply chain, enhancing transparency and accountability. This can help prevent fraud, reduce counterfeiting, and improve efficiency.
- Identity Management: Web3 provides new ways to manage digital identity, giving users more control over their personal information and enabling secure and verifiable authentication.

The Evolution of the Web

Web3 is still in its early stages of development, but it has the potential to transform the internet as we know it. It's an exciting time to be involved in this space, as new applications and technologies are emerging rapidly. By understanding the core principles and potential of Web3, you'll be well-equipped to navigate this evolving landscape and contribute to the future of the internet.

1.2 Key Concepts of Web3

Let's break down the core ideas that make Web3 tick! These concepts might seem a bit abstract at first, but they're the foundation for understanding how this new iteration of the internet works and why it has the potential to be so revolutionary.

1. Blockchain

Imagine a digital ledger that's shared among many computers, recording transactions and data in a secure and transparent way. That's essentially what a blockchain is. It's like a public record book that everyone can access and verify, but no one can tamper with.

Here's a simplified breakdown of how it works:

- Blocks of Data: Transactions and data are grouped into "blocks."
- Chain of Blocks: These blocks are linked together in a chronological "chain," forming a permanent and tamper-proof record.
- Cryptography: Cryptography is used to secure the blockchain, ensuring that data cannot be altered or forged.
- Decentralization: The blockchain is distributed across many computers (nodes), making it resilient to censorship and single points of failure.

Why is blockchain so important for Web3?

- Trust: It creates trust among participants, as everyone has access to the same information and can verify its authenticity.
- Transparency: All transactions are recorded on the blockchain, making them transparent and auditable.
- Security: The cryptographic nature of blockchain makes it extremely secure and resistant to tampering.
- Immutability: Once data is recorded on the blockchain, it cannot be altered or deleted, creating a permanent and auditable history.

Real-world examples:

- Cryptocurrencies: Bitcoin and Ethereum use blockchain technology to record transactions and manage the supply of their respective currencies.
- Supply Chain Management: Companies use blockchain to track goods and materials throughout the supply chain, enhancing transparency and accountability.
- Healthcare: Blockchain can be used to securely store and share medical records, giving patients more control over their data.

2. Decentralization: Distributing Power

Decentralization is the heart and soul of Web3. It's about shifting power and control away from centralized entities like big tech companies and governments, and distributing it among the users.

Why is decentralization important?

- Censorship Resistance: No single entity can control or censor the network.
- Resilience: The network is more resilient to outages and attacks, as there's no single point of failure.

- User Empowerment: Users have more control over their data and interactions.
- Innovation: Decentralization fosters innovation by allowing anyone to participate and contribute.

Real-world examples:

- Decentralized Social Media: Platforms like Mastodon provide an alternative to centralized social media networks, giving users more control over their data and interactions.
- Decentralized File Storage: Services like IPFS (InterPlanetary File System) offer a decentralized way to store and share files, making them more resilient to censorship and data loss.

3. dApps

Decentralized applications (dApps) are applications built on blockchain and other decentralized technologies. They are designed to operate without central control, giving users more autonomy and ownership.

Key characteristics of dApps:

- Open Source: The code is often open source, allowing anyone to inspect and audit it.
- Decentralized Backend: The backend of the application runs on a decentralized network, such as a blockchain.
- Tokenized: Many dApps use tokens to incentivize participation and govern the platform.

Real-world examples:

- Decentralized Exchanges (DEXs): DEXs allow users to trade cryptocurrencies directly with each other without intermediaries.
- NFT Marketplaces: Platforms like OpenSea enable users to buy, sell, and trade NFTs.

- Prediction Markets: Decentralized prediction markets allow users to bet on the outcome of future events.

4. Cryptocurrencies

Cryptocurrencies are digital currencies that use cryptography for security and operate independently of central banks. They are often used as a medium of exchange within Web3 applications.

Key characteristics of cryptocurrencies:

- Decentralized: No single entity controls the issuance or circulation of the currency.
- Secure: Cryptography is used to secure transactions and prevent fraud.
- Transparent: All transactions are recorded on a public blockchain.

Real-world examples:

- Bitcoin: The first and most well-known cryptocurrency.
- Ethereum: A platform for decentralized applications and smart contracts.
- Stablecoins: Cryptocurrencies pegged to the value of stable assets like the US dollar.

5. Smart Contracts

Smart contracts are self-executing contracts with the terms of the agreement directly written into code. They automate transactions and enforce agreements without the need for intermediaries.

Key characteristics of smart contracts:

- Automated: They automatically execute when predefined conditions are met.
- Immutable: Once deployed, the code cannot be altered.
- Transparent: The code is publicly visible on the blockchain.

Real-world examples:

- Decentralized Insurance: Smart contracts can automate insurance claims processing.
- Supply Chain Automation: Smart contracts can track goods and automate payments in supply chains.
- Decentralized Voting: Smart contracts can be used to create secure and transparent voting systems.

By understanding these key concepts, you'll be well-equipped to navigate the world of Web3 and build your own decentralized applications using Solidity.

1.3 The Role of Smart Contracts in Web3

Let's dive deeper into the heart of Web3: smart contracts! These incredible pieces of software are revolutionizing how we think about agreements, transactions, and automation. Think of smart contracts as self-executing agreements with the terms directly written into code. They're like vending machines for the digital age – you provide the input (e.g., payment), and the machine automatically dispenses the output (e.g., the product).

Why are Smart Contracts Important for Web3?

Smart contracts are essential building blocks for many Web3 applications because they offer several key benefits:

- **Automation:** They automate transactions and processes, eliminating the need for intermediaries like lawyers, banks, or escrow services. This reduces costs, speeds up processes, and removes potential points of failure or human error.
- **Trust and Transparency:** Smart contracts are executed on public blockchains, making them transparent and auditable. Anyone can view the code and verify its logic, fostering trust among participants. This transparency also helps prevent fraud and manipulation, as all transactions are recorded on the blockchain.

- **Security:** Smart contracts use cryptography to ensure security and prevent tampering or unauthorized access. Once a smart contract is deployed on the blockchain, its code cannot be altered, guaranteeing the integrity of the agreement.
- **Decentralized Governance:** Smart contracts can be used to create Decentralized Autonomous Organizations (DAOs), where governance rules are encoded in the contract and executed automatically. This allows for decentralized decision-making and eliminates the need for central authorities.

How Smart Contracts Work

Here's a simplified explanation of how smart contracts work:

1. Contract Creation: A developer writes the smart contract code, defining the rules and logic of the agreement. This code is written in a specialized language like Solidity, which we'll learn about in this book.
2. Compilation: The code is compiled into bytecode, a low-level representation that can be executed by the Ethereum Virtual Machine (EVM).
3. Deployment: The compiled bytecode is deployed to the blockchain, where it becomes a permanent and immutable part of the ledger.
4. Execution: When the predefined conditions of the contract are met (e.g., a certain amount of cryptocurrency is transferred), the contract's code is automatically executed by the EVM. This execution might involve transferring funds, updating data on the blockchain, or triggering other actions.

Real-World Examples of Smart Contracts in Action

- Decentralized Exchanges (DEXs): DEXs use smart contracts to facilitate the exchange of cryptocurrencies without the need for centralized exchanges. Users can trade directly with each other, and the smart contract handles the exchange of tokens and ensures that the transaction is secure and fair.
- NFT Marketplaces: NFT marketplaces use smart contracts to manage the ownership and transfer of NFTs. The smart contract ensures that each NFT is unique and that ownership is properly transferred when a sale occurs.
- Decentralized Insurance: Smart contracts can be used to create decentralized insurance platforms where claims are processed automatically based on predefined conditions. For example, a flight insurance contract could automatically pay out compensation if a flight is delayed or canceled, based on data from a reliable source.
- Supply Chain Management: Smart contracts can be used to track goods and materials throughout the supply chain, enhancing transparency and accountability. For example, a smart contract could track the origin and movement of a product from the manufacturer to the consumer, ensuring that it meets quality standards and preventing counterfeiting.
- Decentralized Voting: Smart contracts can be used to create secure and transparent voting systems. The contract can ensure that only eligible voters can cast their votes, that votes are counted accurately, and that the results are tamper-proof.

Code Example (Conceptual):

Solidity

```
// A simple smart contract for transferring Ether
contract EtherTransfer {
```

```solidity
    // Address of the recipient
    address public recipient;
    // Constructor to set the recipient address
    constructor(address _recipient) {
        recipient = _recipient;
    }
    // Function to receive Ether
    receive() external payable {
        // Transfer the received Ether to the recipient
        payable(recipient).transfer(msg.value);
    }
}
```

This simple contract demonstrates how a smart contract can automate a transaction. When someone sends Ether to this contact's address, the receive() function is automatically executed, transferring the received Ether to the specified recipient address.

Exercise:

Try modifying this contract to add a condition that only allows transfers above a certain amount. This will give you a taste of how smart contracts can encode complex logic and automate transactions based on specific rules.

By understanding the role of smart contracts in Web3, you're gaining a deeper appreciation for the power and potential of this technology. Smart contracts are transforming how we think about agreements, automation, and trust in the digital age. They are the engines that drive many decentralized applications, enabling new forms of interaction and collaboration that were not possible before.

1.4 Why Solidity?

Think of it like choosing a tool for a specific job. You wouldn't use a hammer to tighten a screw, right? Similarly, Solidity is specifically designed for writing smart contracts, making it the most suitable and efficient tool for the job.

1. Ethereum Compatibility

Solidity is the native language of the Ethereum Virtual Machine (EVM). The EVM is like the engine that powers the Ethereum blockchain, executing the code of smart contracts. Solidity was created specifically to target the EVM, making it the most compatible and efficient language for writing smart contracts on Ethereum.

It's like speaking the native language of a country – you can communicate more effectively and understand the nuances of the culture better. Similarly, using Solidity allows you to interact with the EVM more directly and efficiently, taking full advantage of its features and capabilities.

2. Turing-Completeness

Solidity is a Turing-complete language. This means it can be used to express any computable function, giving you the flexibility to create a wide range of smart contract logic. You're not limited to simple transactions or predefined operations – you can implement complex algorithms, decision-making processes, and custom functionalities within your smart contracts.

It's like having a versatile set of tools that can be used to build anything you can imagine. You're not limited to prefabricated structures – you can design and build custom creations that meet your specific needs.

3. Object-Oriented Programming

Solidity supports object-oriented programming (OOP) concepts like inheritance and polymorphism. This allows you to structure your code in a modular and reusable way, making it easier to manage and maintain complex smart contracts.

Inheritance allows you to create new contracts that inherit properties and functions from existing contracts, promoting code reuse and reducing redundancy. Polymorphism allows you to define functions that can operate on different types of data, making your code more flexible and adaptable.

It's like building with modular blocks – you can create different structures by combining and reusing the same basic building blocks, making the construction process more efficient and organized.

4. Static Typing

Solidity is statically typed, meaning that the type of each variable is checked at compile time. This helps prevent errors and makes the code more robust. If you try to use a variable in a way that's not compatible with its type, the compiler will catch the error before the contract is deployed, preventing potential bugs and vulnerabilities.

It's like having a spell checker that catches typos before you send an important email. It helps you avoid embarrassing mistakes and ensures that your message is clear and accurate.

5. Large Community and Ecosystem

Solidity has a large and active community of developers, providing ample resources, libraries, and tools to support your development efforts. You can find tutorials, documentation, forums, and open-source projects that can help you learn Solidity, troubleshoot problems, and collaborate with other developers.

It's like being part of a vibrant city with a diverse community of people who can offer support, share knowledge, and collaborate on projects. You're not alone on your journey – there's a whole community ready to help you succeed.

Real-world examples:

- **Aave:** Aave is a decentralized lending and borrowing platform built on Solidity. It allows users to lend and borrow cryptocurrencies without intermediaries, using smart contracts to manage the lending process and ensure security.
- **CryptoKitties:** CryptoKitties is a popular blockchain game that uses Solidity to create unique digital cats that can be bred and traded. It was one of the first mainstream applications of NFTs, demonstrating the potential of Solidity for creating innovative and engaging decentralized applications.
- **Chainlink:** Chain Link provides a decentralized oracle network that connects smart contracts to real-world data. It uses Solidity to create secure and reliable data feeds that can be used by various decentralized applications.

Exercise:

Try writing a simple Solidity contract that stores a value and allows you to retrieve it. This will give you a basic understanding of Solidity syntax and how to interact with the EVM. You can use an online Solidity compiler like Remix to write, compile, and deploy your contract.

By learning Solidity, you're gaining a powerful tool for building decentralized applications and participating in the exciting world of Web3. It's a language that's specifically designed for smart contract development, offering compatibility with the EVM, flexibility, object-oriented features, static typing, and a supportive community. With Solidity, you can unlock the full potential of blockchain technology and contribute to the future of the internet.

Chapter 2: Getting Started with Solidity

It's time to get our hands dirty and start writing some Solidity code! In this chapter, we'll set up your development environment, explore the basic syntax and data types of Solidity, write your first smart contract, and learn how to compile and deploy it using the Remix IDE.

2.1 Setting Up Your Development Environment

Before we can start coding, we need to set up a comfortable and efficient workspace. This involves installing the necessary tools and choosing an Integrated Development Environment (IDE) that suits your preferences.

2.1.1 Installing Necessary Tools

Before we embark on our Solidity coding adventure, we need to set up our development environment. Think of this as preparing your workshop with all the necessary tools and equipment before starting a crafting project. In the world of Solidity development, these "tools" are software applications that will help you write, compile, test, and deploy your smart contracts.

Here's a breakdown of the essential tools we'll be using:

1. Node.js and npm

Node.js is a JavaScript runtime environment that allows you to run JavaScript code outside of a web browser. It's like having a JavaScript interpreter that can run on your computer, independent of any browser. This is essential because many of the tools we'll be using for Solidity development are written in JavaScript.

npm (Node Package Manager) is a tool that comes bundled with Node.js. It's like a vast online store where you can find and download thousands of packages (libraries and tools) for your JavaScript projects. We'll use npm to install the other necessary tools for Solidity development.

Installing Node.js and npm

- Go to the official Node.js website: https://nodejs.org/
- Download the installer for your operating system (Windows, macOS, or Linux).
- Run the installer and follow the on-screen instructions.
- Once the installation is complete, you can verify that Node.js and npm are installed correctly by opening your terminal or command prompt and running the following commands:

<!-- end list -->

Bash

```
node -v
```

```
npm -v
```

These commands should [1] display the version numbers of Node.js and npm, respectively.

2. Truffle Suite

Truffle is a popular development framework specifically designed for Solidity. It provides a suite of tools that make it easier to write, compile, test, and deploy smart contracts. Think of it as a comprehensive toolkit for Solidity developers, providing everything you need to build and manage your smart contracts.

Installing Truffle

You can install Truffle using npm by running the following command in your terminal or command prompt:

Bash

```
npm install -g truffle
```

The -g flag installs Truffle globally, making it accessible from any directory on your system.

Key Features of Truffle

- Contract Compilation: Truffle automates the process of compiling your Solidity code into bytecode, which can be executed by the EVM.
- Testing Framework: Truffle provides a testing framework for writing automated tests for your smart contracts, helping you ensure their correctness and security.
- Deployment Management: Truffle simplifies the deployment of your contracts to various Ethereum networks, including local test networks and public networks.
- Dependency Management: Truffle helps you manage the dependencies of your project, ensuring that you have the correct versions of libraries and packages.

3. Ganache

Ganache is a personal blockchain emulator that allows you to develop and test your smart contracts locally without incurring real gas costs. It creates a simulated Ethereum environment on your computer, providing you with a private blockchain where you can deploy and interact with your contracts without having to connect to a real network.

Think of it as a sandbox where you can play around with your smart contracts without worrying about the costs or complexities of the real Ethereum network.

Installing Ganache

You can download Ganache from the Truffle Suite website: https://trufflesuite.com/ganache/

Key Features of Ganache

- Local Blockchain: Ganache provides a local blockchain instance that you can use for development and testing.
- Accounts and Ether: It automatically creates a set of test accounts with pre-funded Ether balances, allowing you to simulate transactions and interactions.
- Debugging Tools: Ganache offers debugging tools that can help you identify and fix issues in your smart contracts.
- Network Configuration: You can customize the network settings, such as block gas limit and network ID, to match your development needs.

Why Use Ganache?

- Cost-Effective: You can develop and test your contracts without spending real Ether on gas fees.
- Fast and Efficient: Ganache runs locally on your computer, providing a fast and efficient development environment.
- Isolated Environment: You can experiment with your contracts in an isolated environment without affecting the real Ethereum network.
- Debugging: Ganache provides tools to help you debug your contracts and identify potential issues.

By installing these essential tools, you're setting up a solid foundation for your Solidity development journey. They provide the necessary infrastructure for writing, compiling, testing, and deploying your smart contracts, making the development process smoother and more efficient.

2.1.2 Choosing an IDE

Think of an IDE as a chef's kitchen. It has all the necessary tools and appliances organized in a convenient way, making it easier to prepare delicious meals. Similarly, an IDE provides you with the tools and features you need to write clean, efficient, and error-free code.

Key Features of an IDE

Here are some key features that you should look for in a Solidity IDE:

- **Code Editor:** A good code editor is the heart of any IDE. It should provide features like syntax highlighting (coloring different parts of the code to improve readability), code completion (suggesting completions for partially typed code), and automatic indentation (formatting your code to make it more organized).
- **Compiler Integration:** The IDE should seamlessly integrate with the Solidity compiler, allowing you to compile your code with a single click or keyboard shortcut. It should also provide clear error messages and warnings to help you identify and fix any issues in your code.
- **Debugger:** A debugger allows you to step through your code line by line, inspect variables, and identify the source of errors. It's like having a magnifying glass to examine your code in detail and understand its behavior.
- **Testing Framework:** The IDE should support a testing framework that allows you to write automated tests for your smart contracts. This helps you ensure that your contracts function correctly and are free of bugs or vulnerabilities.
- **Deployment Tools:** The IDE should provide tools for deploying your smart contracts to various Ethereum

networks, including local test networks and public networks. It should also make it easy to interact with your deployed contracts and test their functionality.

- **Other Useful Features:** Other useful features might include:
    - **Version Control Integration:** Integration with version control systems like Git allows you to track changes to your code and collaborate with others.
    - **Code Navigation:** Features like "Go to Definition" and "Find All References" help you navigate your codebase more efficiently.
    - **Code Refactoring:** Tools for renaming variables, extracting functions, and performing other code transformations can improve the structure and maintainability of your code.
    - **Extensions and Plugins:** Support for extensions and plugins can add additional functionality to the IDE, such as support for different languages, frameworks, or tools.

Popular IDEs for Solidity Development

Here are two popular choices for Solidity development:

1. **Remix IDE:** Remix is a web-based IDE specifically designed for Solidity development. It's a great choice for beginners because it's easy to use, requires no installation, and provides a user-friendly interface. You can access Remix directly in your web browser without needing to install anything.
    - **Key Features:**
        - Web-based, no installation required.
        - User-friendly interface.
        - Integrated compiler and debugger.
        - Built-in testing framework.
        - Deployment tools for various networks.

- Plugin support for additional functionality.
    - **Access Remix:** https://remix.ethereum.org/
2. **VS Code:** VS Code is a popular and versatile code editor that can be used for a wide range of programming languages, including Solidity. It offers a powerful and customizable environment with many extensions and features that can enhance your development workflow.
    - **Key Features:**
        - Lightweight and fast.
        - Powerful code editor with syntax highlighting, code completion, and debugging.
        - Extensive extension ecosystem, including Solidity support.
        - Integrated terminal for running commands and scripts.
        - Customizable interface and themes.
        - Cross-platform support (Windows, macOS, Linux).
    - **Download VS Code:** https://code.visualstudio.com/
    - **Install the Solidity Extension:** Search for "Solidity" in the VS Code extensions marketplace and install the official Solidity extension.

Which IDE Should You Choose?

Both Remix and VS Code are excellent choices for Solidity development. The best choice for you depends on your preferences and experience:

- **Remix:** If you're a beginner or prefer a simple and easy-to-use environment, Remix is a great starting point. It's web-based, so you don't need to install anything, and it provides all the essential tools for Solidity development in a user-friendly interface.

- **VS Code:** If you're more experienced with code editors or prefer a more customizable and powerful environment, VS Code is a great option. It offers a wider range of features and extensions, allowing you to tailor your development workflow to your needs.

Ultimately, the best way to choose an IDE is to try both and see which one you prefer. You can start with Remix to get a feel for Solidity development, and then transition to VS Code if you need more advanced features or customization options.

2.2 Basic Syntax and Data Types

Solidity is a high-level, object-oriented programming language specifically designed for writing smart contracts. It's statically typed, which means that the type of each variable is checked at compile time, helping prevent errors. If you've had any experience with languages like JavaScript or C++, you'll find some familiar elements in Solidity.

Basic Syntax

- **Contracts:** The fundamental building block in Solidity is the contract. It's like a blueprint that defines the structure and behavior of your smart contract. Inside a contract, you'll define variables to store data and functions to perform actions.

Solidity

```solidity
contract MyContract {
    // Contract code goes here
}
```

- **Variables:** Variables are used to store data within your contract. You need to declare the variable's type before using it. Here are some examples:

Solidity

```
uint256 public myNumber = 10;      // Unsigned integer variable

string public myString = "Hello"; // String variable

bool public myBoolean = true;     // Boolean variable

address public myAddress = 0x123...; // Address variable
```

The public keyword makes these variables accessible from outside the contract.

- **Functions:** Functions are blocks of code that perform specific tasks. They can take arguments as input and return values as output.

Solidity

```
function addNumbers(uint256 a, uint256 b) public pure returns (uint256) {

    return a + b;

}
```

This function takes two unsigned integers as input, adds them together, and returns the result. The public keyword allows anyone to call this function. The pure keyword indicates that this function doesn't read or modify the contract's state.

- **Control Flow:** Solidity supports control flow statements like if, else, for, and while to control the execution of your code, just like in other programming languages.

Solidity

```
function checkValue(uint256 x) public pure
returns (string memory) {

    if (x > 10) {

        return "Greater than 10";

    } else if (x < 10) {

        return "Less than 10";

    } else {

        return "Equal to 10";

    }

}
```

Data Types

Solidity offers a variety of data types to represent different kinds of information:

- **Integers:**
    - int: Signed integers (can be positive or negative).
    - uint: Unsigned integers (can only be positive).
    - You can specify the size of the integer in bits, such as uint8 (8 bits), int256 (256 bits), etc.

- **Booleans:**
  - bool: Represents a boolean value (true or false).
- **Strings:**
  - string: Represents a sequence of characters.
- **Addresses:**
  - address: Represents an Ethereum address. This is a 20-byte value that identifies an account on the Ethereum blockchain.
- **Arrays:**
  - fixed-size arrays: Arrays with a predetermined size, such as uint256[10].
  - dynamic-size arrays: Arrays that can grow or shrink in size, such as string[].
- **Structs:**
  - structs: Custom data structures that allow you to group related variables of different types.

Solidity

```solidity
struct Person {
    string name;
    uint256 age;
}
```

- **Mappings:**
  - mappings: Key-value pairs, similar to dictionaries or hash tables in other languages.

Solidity

```solidity
mapping(address => uint256) public balances;
```

- This example defines a mapping called balances that maps Ethereum addresses to unsigned integers. It could be used to store the balances of different users in a token contract.

Example: Putting it Together

Solidity

```
contract MyContract {

    uint256 public myNumber = 10;

    string public myString = "Hello";

    function updateValues(uint256 newNumber, string memory newString) public {

        myNumber = newNumber;

        myString = newString;

    }

}
```

This contract demonstrates the use of variables, functions, and basic syntax. It defines two public variables (myNumber and myString) and a function (updateValues) that allows you to update their values.

Exercise:

Try adding a new function to this contract that takes an address as an argument and stores it in a new state variable.

By understanding these basic syntax and data types, you're laying the foundation for writing more complex and sophisticated smart contracts. It's like learning the basic vocabulary and grammar of a new language – once you master these fundamentals, you'll be able to express yourself more fluently and creatively in the world of Solidity.

2.3 Writing Your First Smart Contract

It's time to create your very first smart contract! This is where the rubber meets the road, and you'll start putting your Solidity knowledge into practice. Think of it like baking your first cake – you have the ingredients (Solidity syntax and data types) and the tools (your development environment), and now you're ready to follow the recipe and create something delicious (a functional smart contract!).

Our First Contract

For our first foray into Solidity, we'll create a simple contract that stores a single integer value. It's a basic example, but it demonstrates the fundamental structure and functionality of a smart contract.

Code:

Solidity

```solidity
pragma solidity ^0.8.0;

contract SimpleStorage {

    uint256 storedData;

    function set(uint256 x) public {

        storedData = x;

    }

    function get() public view returns (uint256)
{
```

```
        return storedData;
```
    }

}

Explanation:

Let's break down this code step-by-step:

- pragma solidity ^0.8.0;: This line is like a header that tells the Solidity compiler which version of the language to use. In this case, we're using version 0.8.0 or any version above it, up to but not including version 0.9.0. This ensures that our code is compiled correctly and uses the intended features of the language.
- contract SimpleStorage { ... }: This defines a contract named SimpleStorage. The curly braces {} enclose the code that belongs to this contract. Think of the contract as a container that holds variables and functions.
- uint256 storedData;: This line declares a state variable named storedData. A state variable is like a piece of information that the contract remembers. In this case, it stores an unsigned integer (a whole number that cannot be negative) of 256 bits. This variable will hold the value that we want to store in our contract.
- function set(uint256 x) public { ... }: This defines a function named set. Functions are like actions that the contract can perform. This particular function takes an unsigned integer (x) as input and stores it in the storedData variable. The public keyword means that this function can be called by anyone (or any other contract).
- function get() public view returns (uint256) { ... }: This defines another function named get. This function doesn't take any input but returns the current value stored in the storedData variable. The public keyword again means that anyone can call this function. The view keyword indicates

that this function doesn't modify the contract's state – it only reads from it.

How This Contract Works

This contract provides a simple way to store and retrieve an integer value on the blockchain. Here's how it works:

1. Deployment: When you deploy this contract to the blockchain, it creates an instance of the SimpleStorage contract with its own storage space.
2. Setting a Value: To store a value, you would call the set() function with the desired integer as an argument. This function updates the storedData variable with the new value.
3. Getting the Value: To retrieve the stored value, you would call the get() function. This function returns the current value of storedData.

Real-World Analogy

Think of this contract as a digital safe deposit box. You can use the set() function to deposit a value (like putting something valuable in the box), and you can use the get() function to retrieve the stored value (like opening the box to see what's inside).

Exercise:

Try modifying this contract to store a string instead of an integer. You'll need to change the data type of the storedData variable to string and update the set() and get() functions accordingly.

This simple contract demonstrates the basic structure and functionality of a Solidity smart contract. It shows how to define variables to store data and functions to perform actions. As you progress through this book, you'll learn how to create more complex and sophisticated contracts that can handle various tasks and interactions.

2.4 Compiling and Deploying with Remix

Now that you've written your first smart contract, let's bring it to life! In this section, we'll use Remix, the online Solidity IDE, to compile and deploy your contract to a simulated blockchain environment. Think of Remix as your virtual laboratory where you can experiment with your smart contracts without incurring any real costs or risks.

Remix

Remix is a powerful and user-friendly IDE that runs entirely in your web browser. It provides all the necessary tools for Solidity development, including a code editor, compiler, debugger, and deployment tools. It's a great choice for beginners because it's easy to use and accessible from any device with an internet connection.

Compiling Your Contract

Before your smart contract can be deployed to the blockchain, it needs to be compiled. Compilation is the process of translating your human-readable Solidity code into bytecode, a low-level representation that the Ethereum Virtual Machine (EVM) can understand and execute. Think of it like translating a recipe from English to a language that your kitchen appliances can understand.

Here's how to compile your contract in Remix:

1. **Open Remix:** Go to the Remix website: https://remix.ethereum.org/
2. Create a New File: Click on the "+" icon in the file explorer pane on the left side of the screen. Name your file SimpleStorage.sol (or whatever you named your contract).

3. Paste Your Code: Copy the code for your SimpleStorage contract and paste it into the new file in Remix.
4. Go to the Solidity Compiler: Click on the "Solidity Compiler" tab in the sidebar. This will open the compiler pane.
5. Select Compiler Version: Make sure the compiler version in Remix matches the version specified in your code (pragma solidity ^0.8.0;). You can select the compiler version from the dropdown menu in the compiler pane.
6. Compile: Click on the "Compile SimpleStorage.sol" button. If there are no errors in your code, Remix will compile your contract and generate the bytecode. You'll see a green checkmark next to the "Compile" button if the compilation is successful.

Deploying Your Contract

Once your contract is compiled, you can deploy it to the blockchain. Deployment is the process of creating an instance of your contract on the blockchain, making it live and accessible to users. Think of it like launching a rocket into space – once it's deployed, it's out there and ready to perform its mission.

Here's how to deploy your contract in Remix:

1. Go to the Deploy & Run Transactions Pane: Click on the "Deploy & Run Transactions" tab in the sidebar.
2. Choose an Environment: In the "Environment" dropdown menu, select "JavaScript VM." This will create a simulated blockchain environment in your browser, allowing you to deploy and test your contract without using real Ether or connecting to a real network.
3. Select Your Contract: Make sure your contract (SimpleStorage) is selected in the "Contract" dropdown menu.

4. Deploy: Click on the "Deploy" button. Remix will deploy your contract to the simulated blockchain. You'll see a transaction record in the console pane at the bottom of the screen, indicating that the deployment was successful.

Interacting with Your Contract

After deploying your contract, you can interact with it using the Remix interface. You'll see your deployed contract listed in the "Deployed Contracts" section of the sidebar.

- Access Contract Functions: Expand the contract in the sidebar to see its functions (set and get).
- Call the set Function: To store a value in your contract, enter a number in the input field next to the set function and click on the "set" button. This will send a transaction to the contract, updating the storedData variable with the value you provided.
- Call the get Function: To retrieve the stored value, click on the "get" button next to the get function. The contract will execute the get function and return the stored value, which will be displayed in the console pane.

Exercise:

Try deploying the modified contract you created in the previous exercise (the one that stores a string). In the "Deploy" section, enter a string value in the _value field (e.g., "Hello, blockchain!"). Deploy the contract and then try calling the getValue function to retrieve the stored string.

By compiling and deploying your contract in Remix, you've taken a crucial step in your Solidity journey. You've seen how to translate your code into bytecode, launch it on a simulated blockchain, and interact with its functions. This hands-on experience will give you a solid foundation for building more complex and sophisticated smart contracts as you progress through this book.

Chapter 3: Understanding the Ethereum Blockchain

In this chapter, we'll explore what Ethereum is, how it works, and the key components that make it tick. We'll also look at different types of Ethereum networks, from the mainnet to testnets, and how to interact with them.

3.1 What is Ethereum?

Think of Ethereum as a global, shared computer that anyone can access and use. It's like a massive, decentralized network of computers working together to maintain a secure and transparent ledger of transactions and data. Unlike traditional computers, which are centralized and controlled by a single entity, Ethereum is distributed across thousands of computers around the world, making it resistant to censorship, tampering, and single points of failure.

Key Features of Ethereum

Here are some key features that make Ethereum a powerful platform for Web3 development:

- **Smart Contracts:** Ethereum is designed to support smart contracts, which are self-executing contracts with the terms of the agreement directly written into code. This allows for the automation of complex transactions and agreements without the need for intermediaries like lawyers or banks. It's like having a digital vending machine that automatically dispenses goods or services when you provide the correct input (e.g., payment).
- **Decentralized Applications (dApps):** Ethereum provides the infrastructure for building dApps, which are applications that run on a decentralized network and offer users more control over their data and interactions. dApps

are often open-source, transparent, and resistant to censorship, making them ideal for building trustless and user-centric applications.
- **Cryptocurrency (Ether):** Ether (ETH) is the native cryptocurrency of the Ethereum blockchain. It's used to pay for transaction fees (gas), which we'll discuss later, and can also be used as a store of value or a medium of exchange within dApps. Think of Ether as the fuel that powers the Ethereum network and enables transactions to occur.
- **Turing-Complete:** The Ethereum Virtual Machine (EVM), which we'll explore in more detail later, is Turing-complete. This means it can theoretically perform any computation that a traditional computer can. This gives developers immense flexibility to create a wide range of complex and sophisticated dApps, from decentralized exchanges and games to supply chain management systems and voting platforms.
- **Large Community and Ecosystem:** Ethereum has a large and active community of developers, researchers, and users, fostering innovation and collaboration. It also has a rich ecosystem of tools, libraries, and resources that support development. This means you'll have plenty of support and resources available as you learn to build dApps on Ethereum.

How Ethereum Works

Here's a simplified explanation of how Ethereum works:

1. **Transactions:** Users send transactions to the Ethereum network to interact with smart contracts, transfer Ether, or deploy new contracts. These transactions are like instructions that tell the network what you want to do.
2. **Blocks:** Transactions are grouped together into blocks. These blocks are like containers that hold a batch of transactions.

3. **Mining:** Miners use their computational power to validate transactions and add new blocks to the blockchain. This process, known as mining, involves solving complex mathematical problems to ensure the security and integrity of the network.
4. **Blockchain:** The blockchain is a growing chain of blocks that records all transactions and data in a chronological and tamper-proof manner. It's like a public ledger that everyone can access and verify, but no one can alter or delete.
5. **Smart Contracts:** Smart contracts are deployed to the blockchain and executed by the EVM when triggered by transactions. They are stored on the blockchain and can be accessed and interacted with by anyone.

Real-World Examples of Ethereum in Action

- **Decentralized Finance (DeFi):** DeFi applications are revolutionizing the financial industry by providing services like lending, borrowing, and trading without intermediaries like banks. Platforms like Aave and Compound allow users to earn interest on their cryptocurrencies or borrow against them, while Uniswap enables decentralized token swaps.
- **Non-Fungible Tokens (NFTs):** NFTs are unique digital assets that represent ownership of digital or physical items. They are used for everything from digital art and collectibles to virtual real estate and in-game items. Platforms like OpenSea and Rarible allow users to create, buy, sell, and trade NFTs.
- **Supply Chain Management:** Companies are using Ethereum to track goods and materials throughout the supply chain, enhancing transparency and accountability. This can help prevent fraud, reduce counterfeiting, and improve efficiency. For example, Walmart uses blockchain to track the origin and movement of its food products.
- **Gaming:** Ethereum is powering a new generation of blockchain-based games that give players true ownership of

in-game assets and allow for new forms of gameplay and interaction. Games like Axie Infinity and Decentraland are creating immersive virtual worlds where players can own land, build structures, and trade assets.
- **Decentralized Identity:** Ethereum is being used to create decentralized identity systems that give users more control over their personal information and enable secure and verifiable authentication. This can help reduce reliance on centralized identity providers and empower users to manage their own digital identities.

By understanding the fundamentals of Ethereum, you're gaining a solid foundation for building your own decentralized applications using Solidity. It's a powerful platform that's driving innovation in many industries and has the potential to transform the way we interact and transact online.

3.2 Accounts, Transactions, and Gas

Let's break down some of the core components that make the Ethereum blockchain tick! Understanding these concepts is like learning the basic rules of a game before you start playing. Once you grasp these fundamentals, you'll be well-equipped to navigate the Ethereum landscape and interact with smart contracts effectively.

Accounts

In the world of Ethereum, every participant has an account. Think of an account as your digital identity on the blockchain. It's similar to a bank account, but instead of just holding money, it can hold various types of digital assets, such as:

- **Ether (ETH):** The native cryptocurrency of Ethereum.

- **Tokens:** Other cryptocurrencies or digital assets that are built on top of Ethereum, such as ERC-20 tokens (we'll learn more about these later!).
- **NFTs:** Non-fungible tokens that represent unique digital or physical items.

Each account has a unique address, which is a long string of alphanumeric characters. This address is like your account number, and you can use it to send and receive digital assets.

Types of Accounts

There are two main types of accounts in Ethereum:

- **Externally Owned Accounts (EOAs):** These are controlled by users like you and me. They are secured by a private key, which is like a secret password that only you know. You use your private key to authorize transactions and prove ownership of your account.
- **Contract Accounts:** These are controlled by smart contract code. They don't have a private key and are automatically managed by the code of the contract. When someone interacts with a smart contract, they are essentially interacting with its contract account.

Transactions

A transaction is a request to change the state of the Ethereum blockchain. It's like an instruction that you send to the network to perform a specific action. This action could be:

- **Transferring Ether:** Sending Ether from one account to another.
- **Interacting with a Smart Contract:** Calling a function on a smart contract to execute its code.
- **Deploying a New Contract:** Creating a new smart contract and adding it to the blockchain.

Each transaction is recorded on the blockchain, creating a permanent and tamper-proof record of all activity.

Gas

Every transaction on the Ethereum network requires computational effort to process. This effort is measured in a unit called "gas." Think of gas as the fuel that powers the Ethereum engine.

When you send a transaction, you need to include a gas fee, which is paid in Ether. This fee incentivizes miners to validate your transaction and include it in a block. It also helps prevent spam and denial-of-service attacks by making it costly to flood the network with frivolous transactions.

Gas Limit and Gas Price

Each transaction has a gas limit, which is the maximum amount of gas you're willing to spend on that transaction. If the transaction requires more gas than the limit, it will fail.

The gas price is the amount of Ether you're willing to pay per unit of gas. Higher gas prices incentivize miners to prioritize your transaction, leading to faster processing times.

Managing Gas Costs

Gas fees can fluctuate depending on network congestion and the complexity of the transaction. When the network is busy, gas fees tend to be higher.

Here are some ways to manage gas costs:

- **Adjust gas limits:** You can set a gas limit that's appropriate for the complexity of your transaction.

- **Monitor gas prices:** You can use tools and websites to track current gas prices and choose a time when fees are lower.
- **Optimize your code:** You can write efficient smart contract code to minimize the amount of gas required for execution.

Real-world analogy:

Imagine sending a package through a courier service. The package is your transaction, the courier service is the Ethereum network, and the shipping fee is the gas fee. The shipping fee depends on the size and weight of the package (complexity of the transaction) and the distance it needs to travel (network congestion).

Example:

When you deploy a smart contract to the Ethereum network, you're initiating a transaction. This transaction includes the contract's bytecode and requires a certain amount of gas to be processed. You pay for this gas using Ether, and the miners will include your transaction in a block once it's validated.

By understanding accounts, transactions, and gas, you're gaining a deeper understanding of how the Ethereum blockchain works and how to interact with it effectively. These concepts are fundamental to building and deploying smart contracts and decentralized applications.

3.3 Ethereum Virtual Machine (EVM)

Let's take a closer look at the engine that powers the Ethereum blockchain: the Ethereum Virtual Machine (EVM). Think of the EVM as a global, decentralized computer that executes the code of smart contracts. It's like a virtual machine that runs on every node in the Ethereum network, ensuring that contracts are executed consistently and securely no matter where in the world they're being accessed.

What is the EVM?

The EVM is a sandboxed runtime environment that provides a secure and isolated space for executing smart contracts. It's designed to prevent contracts from interfering with each other or with the underlying operating system of the nodes on which they run. This isolation is crucial for security and stability, as it prevents malicious or buggy contracts from harming the network or other users.

Think of it like this: each smart contract runs in its own little compartment within the EVM. These compartments are completely sealed off from each other, preventing any interference or cross-contamination. This ensures that each contract can operate independently and securely without affecting others.

Key Features of the EVM

- **Turing-Complete:** The EVM is Turing-complete, meaning it can theoretically perform any computation that a traditional computer can. This gives developers immense flexibility to create a wide range of complex and sophisticated smart contracts, from simple token transfers to complex decentralized applications.
- **Stack-Based:** The EVM uses a stack-based architecture, where data and instructions are stored on a stack. This is a common architecture for virtual machines, and it's efficient for executing the type of code typically found in smart contracts, which often involves manipulating data and performing calculations.
- **Secure and Isolated:** As mentioned earlier, the EVM provides a secure and isolated environment for executing smart contracts. This prevents malicious code from harming

the network or other users and ensures that contracts can only access their own data and resources.
- **Deterministic:** The EVM is deterministic, meaning that given the same input, it will always produce the same output. This is crucial for ensuring that contracts are executed consistently across all nodes in the network, maintaining the integrity of the blockchain.

How the EVM Works

Here's a simplified explanation of how the EVM executes a smart contract:

1. **Transaction Triggers Execution:** When a user sends a transaction that interacts with a smart contract, the EVM is invoked to execute the contract's code.
2. **Bytecode Loading:** The EVM loads the contract's bytecode, which is the compiled version of the Solidity code.
3. **Stack Operations:** The EVM uses a stack to store data and perform operations. Instructions in the bytecode push and pop data from the stack, perform calculations, and access the contract's storage.
4. **State Changes:** As the EVM executes the code, it can modify the state of the blockchain, such as updating account balances, storing data in the contract's storage, or creating new contracts.
5. **Gas Consumption:** Each operation performed by the EVM consumes a certain amount of gas, which is paid for by the user who initiated the transaction. This gas mechanism prevents infinite loops and resource exhaustion attacks.

Real-World Analogy

Imagine a secure data center with many servers, each running its own isolated program. The data center is the Ethereum network, the servers are the nodes, and the programs are the smart contracts. The EVM is like the operating system that manages the execution of these programs, ensuring that they run securely and independently of each other.

Understanding the EVM's Role

The EVM is a crucial component of the Ethereum blockchain. It provides the runtime environment for smart contracts, ensuring that they are executed consistently, securely, and efficiently. By understanding how the EVM works, you can write better smart contracts that optimize for gas usage and avoid potential vulnerabilities.

Example:

When you deploy a contract in Remix using the "JavaScript VM" environment, you're essentially using a simulated EVM that runs within your browser. This allows you to test and debug your contracts without interacting with the real Ethereum network.

As you delve deeper into Solidity and smart contract development, you'll gain a more profound appreciation for the EVM's role in enabling the decentralized applications that are shaping the future of the internet.

3.4 Exploring the Ethereum Network (Mainnet, Testnets)

Let's explore the different environments where your Solidity smart contracts can live! Just like there are different types of roads – highways, local roads, and private test tracks – there are different types of Ethereum networks, each serving a specific purpose.

Mainnet

The mainnet is the primary Ethereum network, the "real deal" where real Ether (ETH) is used and real transactions occur. It's like the bustling highway system of the Ethereum world, where most of the traffic flows and where the majority of dApps and smart contracts are deployed for actual use.

Why use the mainnet?

- **Real-world deployment:** If you want your dApp or smart contract to be used by real users and interact with real Ether, you need to deploy it on the mainnet. It's like opening a store on a busy street where customers can come in and purchase your goods or services.
- **Access to the full ecosystem:** The mainnet is where the full Ethereum ecosystem exists, including all the dApps, tokens, and users. It's like being part of a vibrant city with a diverse community and a thriving economy.

Things to keep in mind about the mainnet:

- **Gas costs:** Every transaction on the mainnet requires gas, which is paid for in Ether. These gas fees can be significant, especially during periods of high network congestion. It's like paying rent for your store on that busy street – the more popular the location, the higher the rent.
- **Immutability:** Once you deploy a contract to the mainnet, its code becomes immutable, meaning it cannot be changed. This highlights the importance of thorough testing and auditing before deploying to the mainnet. It's like setting the foundation of your store – once it's set, it's difficult and expensive to make changes.

Testnets

Testnets are simulated Ethereum environments that allow you to experiment and test your smart contracts without using real Ether. They're like the driving school of the Ethereum world, where you can practice your skills and test your code without the risk of crashing or causing damage.

Why use testnets?

- **Cost-effective testing:** You can deploy and test your contracts without spending real Ether on gas fees. It's like practicing your driving skills in a simulator before hitting the real road – you can make mistakes without incurring real costs.
- **Safe experimentation:** You can experiment with different configurations and scenarios without affecting the mainnet or risking real funds. It's like trying out different driving techniques in a safe environment without worrying about getting into an accident.
- **Debugging and troubleshooting:** Testnets provide a safe environment to identify and fix bugs in your code before deploying it to the mainnet. It's like taking your car to a mechanic for a test drive before a long road trip – you can identify and fix any issues before they become major problems.

Popular Testnets

There are several popular testnets available for Ethereum development:

- **Goerli:** A popular testnet that closely mimics the mainnet environment. It's widely used by developers and considered a good representation of the real Ethereum network.
- **Sepolia:** Another widely used testnet that's suitable for testing dApps and smart contracts. It's known for its stability and reliability.
- **Holesky:** A newer testnet that's designed for client and protocol developers. It offers a more controlled environment for testing specific features and upgrades.

Choosing the Right Network

The choice of network depends on your needs and goals:

- **Development and testing:** Use a testnet like Goerli or Sepolia for development and testing. This allows you to experiment and iterate quickly without incurring real costs.
- **Real-world deployment:** Use the mainnet for deploying your dApp or smart contract for actual use by real users.

Accessing Ethereum Networks

You can access Ethereum networks through various methods:

- **Web3 Providers:** Services like Infura and Alchemy provide access to Ethereum nodes, allowing you to interact with the blockchain without running your own node. They act like gateways to the Ethereum network, providing you with the infrastructure you need to connect and interact with the blockchain.
- **MetaMask:** MetaMask is a popular browser extension that acts as a wallet and allows you to connect to different Ethereum networks. It's like your digital passport that allows you to access different parts of the Ethereum world.
- **Command-line tools:** Tools like geth and parity allow you to run your own Ethereum node and interact with the network through the command line. This gives you more control over your node and allows you to participate in the network more directly.

Example:

When you deploy a contract in Remix using the "JavaScript VM" environment, you're essentially using a local testnet that's simulated within your browser. This provides a quick and easy way to test your contracts without any external dependencies.

By understanding the different types of Ethereum networks and how to access them, you're gaining the knowledge to navigate the Ethereum ecosystem and choose the right environment for your development and deployment needs. It's like having a map of the Ethereum world, allowing you to choose the best route to reach your destination.

Chapter 4: Core Solidity Concepts

In this chapter, we'll delve into the core concepts that will empower you to write powerful and versatile smart contracts. Think of it as learning the essential tools and techniques of a master craftsman – once you master these concepts, you'll be able to create intricate and sophisticated designs in the world of decentralized applications.

4.1 Functions and Modifiers

Let's discuss the dynamic duo of Solidity: functions and modifiers! These are essential tools in your smart contract toolkit, allowing you to define actions and control the flow of your code. Think of functions as the verbs in a sentence, describing what your contract *does*, and modifiers as the adverbs, adding extra conditions or nuances to those actions.

Functions

A function is a self-contained block of code that performs a specific task. It's like a mini-program within your smart contract. You can give a function a name, provide it with some input (arguments), and it will process that input to produce an output (return value) or modify the contract's state.

Here's a simple example of a function that adds two numbers:

Solidity

```solidity
function add(uint256 a, uint256 b) public pure returns (uint256) {

   return a + b;

}
```

Let's break it down:

- function add(uint256 a, uint256 b): This declares a function named add that takes two arguments, a and b, both of type uint256 (unsigned integers of 256 bits).
- public: This keyword specifies that the function can be called by anyone, including external users or other contracts.
- pure: This keyword indicates that the function doesn't read or modify the contract's state. It only performs calculations with the provided input.
- returns (uint256): This specifies that the function returns a value of type uint256.
- return a + b;: This line performs the addition and returns the result.

Function Visibility

Solidity provides different visibility specifiers for functions, controlling who can call them:

- public: Anyone can call the function. This is the most permissive visibility.
- private: Only the contract itself can call the function. This is the most restrictive visibility.
- internal: The function can be called by the contract itself or by contracts that inherit from it (we'll discuss inheritance later). This is a common visibility for functions that are used internally within a contract or a family of related contracts.
- external: The function can only be called from outside the contract. This is often used for functions that are meant to be interacted with by external users or contracts.

Function Overloading

Solidity allows you to define multiple functions with the same name but with different arguments. This is called function overloading. The compiler will determine which function to call based on the types and number of arguments provided.

Solidity

```
function greet(string memory name) public pure
returns (string memory) {

   return string(abi.encodePacked("Hello, ", name,
"!"));

}

function greet(uint256 age) public pure returns
(string memory) {

   return string(abi.encodePacked("You are ",
Strings.toString(age), " years old."));

}
```

In this example, we have two greet functions. One takes a string (name) as input, and the other takes an unsigned integer (age).

Modifiers

Modifiers are like special functions that can be used to modify the behavior of other functions. They are typically used to add pre-conditions, post-conditions, or checks before a function executes.

Here's an example of a modifier that checks if the caller of a function is the owner of the contract:

Solidity

```
modifier onlyOwner() {

   require(msg.sender == owner, "Only the owner
can call this function.");

   _;
```

}

```
function changeOwner(address newOwner) public
onlyOwner {

  owner = newOwner;

}
```

In this code:

- modifier onlyOwner() { ... }: This declares a modifier named onlyOwner.
- require(msg.sender == owner, "Only the owner can call this function.");: This line checks if the msg.sender (the address of the caller) is equal to the owner of the contract. If not, it throws an error with the provided message.
- _;: This underscore represents the code of the function that the modifier is applied to.

The changeOwner function has the onlyOwner modifier applied to it. This means that the code inside the onlyOwner modifier will be executed before the code inside the changeOwner function. If the require statement in the modifier fails, the changeOwner function will not be executed.

Real-world examples:

- **Access Control:** Modifiers can be used to restrict access to certain functions, like in the onlyOwner example above. This is common in token contracts, where only the owner might be allowed to mint new tokens or change certain parameters.
- **Input Validation:** Modifiers can be used to validate input arguments, ensuring that they meet certain criteria before the function executes. For example, a modifier could check if a transferred amount is greater than zero.

- **State Changes:** Modifiers can be used to perform actions before or after a function executes, such as updating a counter or emitting an event.

Exercise:

Try creating a modifier that checks if a certain condition is true (e.g., if a balance is sufficient) before allowing a function to execute.

By understanding functions and modifiers, you're gaining powerful tools for structuring and controlling the behavior of your smart contracts. They allow you to define actions, add constraints, and ensure that your contracts execute in a secure and predictable manner.

4.2 Variables and Data Structures

Let's talk about how to manage information within your smart contracts! In Solidity, we use variables to store data, and we use data structures to organize and represent that data in meaningful ways. Think of variables as the individual ingredients in a recipe, and data structures as the ways you combine those ingredients to create a delicious dish.

Variables

In Solidity, a variable is like a container that holds a piece of information. You can give each variable a name, and you can store different types of data in them, such as numbers, text, or addresses.

Declaring Variables

Before you can use a variable, you need to declare it. This tells the compiler the name of the variable and the type of data it will hold. Here's the basic syntax:

Solidity

```
// Syntax:

// <data type> <visibility specifier> <variable name>;

// Examples:

uint256 public myNumber;        // Unsigned integer

string private myName;          // String

bool internal isComplete;       // Boolean

address payable public owner;   // Payable address
```

Let's break down the components of a variable declaration:

- **Data Type:** This specifies the kind of data the variable will hold. Solidity offers various data types, which we'll explore shortly.
- **Visibility Specifier:** This determines who can access the variable.
  - public: The variable can be accessed from anywhere (inside and outside the contract).
  - private: The variable can only be accessed from within the contract itself.
  - internal: The variable can be accessed from within the contract and from contracts that inherit from it.
- **Variable Name:** This is the name you give to the variable, which you'll use to refer to it in your code.

Solidity Data Types

Solidity provides a range of data types to represent different kinds of information:

- **Value Types:** These types hold the data directly within the variable itself.
    - **Booleans (**bool**):** Represents a true or false value.
    - **Integers (**int **and** uint**):** Represent whole numbers. int can be positive or negative, while uint can only be positive (unsigned). You can specify the size of the integer in bits, such as uint8 (8 bits), int256 (256 bits), etc.
    - **Fixed-Point Numbers (**fixed **and** unfixed**):** Represent numbers with a fractional component. However, these are not fully supported in all versions of Solidity and are generally less commonly used.
    - **Address (**address**):** Represents an Ethereum address. This is a 20-byte value that identifies an account on the Ethereum blockchain. You can use the payable keyword with address to indicate that the address can receive Ether.
    - **Enums (**enum**):** Define a type that can have one of several predefined values.
    - **Bytes (**bytes **to** bytes32**):** Fixed-size byte arrays.
    - **Dynamically-Sized Byte Array (**bytes**):** A byte array that can grow or shrink in size.
    - **String (**string**):** Represents a sequence of characters.
- **Reference Types:** These types store a reference to the data, rather than the data itself.
    - **Arrays (**[]**):** Ordered collections of elements of the same type. Arrays can be fixed-size (e.g., uint256[10]) or dynamic-size (e.g., string[]).
    - **Structs (**struct**):** Custom data structures that allow you to group related variables of different types.
    - **Mappings (**mapping**):** Key-value pairs, similar to dictionaries or hash tables in other languages.

Data Structures

Data structures allow you to organize and represent data in a structured way. Here are some common data structures in Solidity:

- **Arrays:** Arrays are used to store collections of elements of the same type. For example, you could use an array to store a list of names, a set of numbers, or a collection of addresses.

Solidity

```
string[] public names;   // Dynamically-sized array of strings

uint256[5] public numbers; // Fixed-size array of 5 unsigned integers
```

- **Structs:** Structs allow you to define custom data structures that group related variables of different types. For example, you could use a struct to represent a person with properties like name, age, and address.

Solidity

```
struct Person {

    string name;

    uint256 age;

    address payable account;

}

Person public person1; // Create an instance of the Person struct
```

- **Mappings:** Mappings are used to store key-value pairs. They are similar to dictionaries or hash tables in other languages. For example, you could use a mapping to store the balances of different users in a token contract.

Solidity

```
mapping(address => uint256) public balances;
```

- In this example, the keys are Ethereum addresses, and the values are unsigned integers representing balances.

Real-World Examples

- **ERC-20 Tokens:** ERC-20 tokens, a standard for fungible tokens on Ethereum, use mappings to store the balances of token holders.
- **NFT Marketplaces:** NFT marketplaces use structs to represent NFTs, storing properties like the token ID, owner address, and metadata URI.
- **Decentralized Exchanges:** DEXs use arrays to store order books, which are lists of buy and sell orders for different tokens.

Exercise:

Try creating a contract that uses a struct to represent a product with properties like name, price, and quantity. Add functions to add new products and update their properties.

By understanding variables and data structures in Solidity, you're gaining the ability to manage and represent information effectively within your smart contracts. This is essential for building complex and sophisticated dApps that can handle various types of data and interactions.

4.3 Control Flow and Error Handling

Think of control flow like the traffic signals and road signs that guide the flow of vehicles on a road network. They determine which paths the vehicles can take, when to stop, and when to go. Error handling is like having emergency services and roadside assistance ready to handle accidents or breakdowns, ensuring that traffic can continue to flow smoothly.

Control Flow Statements

Solidity provides several control flow statements that allow you to control the execution of your code:

- **if and else:** These statements allow you to execute different blocks of code based on a condition. It's like a fork in the road – if the condition is true, you take one path; otherwise, you take another.

Solidity

```solidity
function checkValue(uint256 x) public pure returns (string memory) {

    if (x > 10) {

        return "Greater than 10";

    } else if (x < 10) {

        return "Less than 10";

    } else {

        return "Equal to 10";

    }

}
```

- In this example, the checkValue function checks the value of x and returns a different string based on whether it's greater than, less than, or equal to 10.
- **for loop:** This statement allows you to repeat a block of code a specific number of times. It's like driving around a circular track with a set number of laps.

Solidity

```
function sumNumbers(uint256 n) public pure
returns (uint256) {

    uint256 sum = 0;

    for (uint256 i = 1; i <= n; i++) {

        sum += i;

    }

    return sum;

}
```

- This sumNumbers function calculates the sum of numbers from 1 to n using a for loop.
- **while loop:** This statement allows you to repeat a block of code as long as a condition is true. It's like driving until you reach your destination.

Solidity

```
function findFactorial(uint256 n) public pure
returns (uint256) {

    uint256 result = 1;

    while (n > 1) {
```

```
        result *= n;

        n--;

    }

    return result;

}
```

- This findFactorial function calculates the factorial of a number using a while loop.

Error Handling

Error handling is crucial in smart contract development. It allows you to gracefully handle unexpected situations, prevent your contract from crashing, and provide informative error messages to users.

Solidity provides several mechanisms for error handling:

- **require:** This statement checks a condition and throws an error if the condition is not met. It's like a security guard at a door, checking if you have the required credentials before allowing you to enter.

Solidity

```
function transfer(address to, uint256 amount) public {

    require(balances[msg.sender] >= amount, "Insufficient balance.");

    // ... transfer logic ...

}
```

- In this example, the required statement checks if the sender has sufficient balance before allowing the transfer to proceed. If the balance is insufficient, it throws an error with the message "Insufficient balance."
- assert: This statement is similar to require, but it's used for internal checks within the contract's logic. It's like a safety check within a machine, ensuring that all internal components are functioning correctly. If an assert statement fails, it indicates a bug in the contract's code.

Solidity

```solidity
function calculateBonus(uint256 sales) public pure returns (uint256) {

    uint256 bonus = sales * 10 / 100;

    assert(bonus <= sales); // Ensure the bonus is not greater than the sales

    return bonus;

}
```

- revert: This statement stops the execution of the current function and reverts any state changes that were made. It's like hitting the "undo" button, restoring the contract's state to its previous condition.

Solidity

```solidity
function processPayment(uint256 amount) public {

    // ... some logic ...

    if (paymentFailed) {

        revert("Payment failed.");
```

```
    }
    // ... continue processing ...
}
```

Real-World Examples

- **Access Control:** Control flow statements are used to implement access control in smart contracts, such as checking if a user has the necessary permissions to perform an action.
- **Token Transfers:** Error handling is crucial in token contracts to prevent invalid transfers, such as transferring more tokens than a user owns or transferring tokens to an invalid address.
- **Decentralized Exchanges:** DEXs use control flow and error handling to manage order books, match buy and sell orders, and prevent fraudulent or erroneous trades.

Exercise:

Try writing a function that takes two addresses and an amount as input and transfers tokens from one address to another. Use `require` statements to ensure that the sender has sufficient balance and that the recipient address is valid.

By understanding control flow and error handling in Solidity, you're gaining the ability to write more robust and reliable smart contracts. You can now implement complex logic, handle unexpected situations, and prevent your contracts from crashing or behaving unpredictably.

4.4 Events and Logging

Think of events as your contract sending out announcements or notifications whenever something interesting happens. It's like a news broadcast that informs the world about important events, such as a new token being transferred or a proposal being voted on. Logging, on the other hand, is like keeping a diary or a logbook, recording internal details about the contract's execution for debugging and analysis.

Events

Events allow your smart contract to emit information that can be captured and processed by off-chain applications. This is crucial for building interactive dApps, as it allows external applications to react to events happening on the blockchain.

For example, a decentralized exchange (DEX) might emit an event whenever a trade occurs, allowing front-end applications to update their order books and display the latest trades to users.

Declaring and Emitting Events

To use events in Solidity, you first need to declare them using the event keyword:

Solidity

```solidity
event Transfer(address indexed from, address indexed to, uint256 amount);
```

This declares an event called Transfer that includes three parameters: the address of the sender (from), the address of the recipient (to), and the amount transferred (amount). The indexed keyword allows you to filter events based on these parameters, making it easier to search for specific events later.

To emit an event, you use the emit keyword:

Solidity

```solidity
function transfer(address to, uint256 amount) public {
    // ... transfer logic ...
```

```
    emit Transfer(msg.sender, to, amount);
}
```

In this example, the transfer function emits the Transfer event after successfully transferring tokens. This event will be recorded on the blockchain and can be picked up by off-chain applications that are listening for it.

Benefits of Using Events

- **Transparency:** Events provide a transparent record of what's happening within your contract, making it easier for users and developers to understand its behavior.
- **Interactivity:** Events enable interactive dApps by allowing off-chain applications to react to on-chain events in real time.
- **Efficiency:** Events are an efficient way to communicate information off-chain, as they only include the necessary data and avoid unnecessary computations.

Real-World Examples

- **ERC-20 Tokens:** The ERC-20 token standard defines several events, such as Transfer and Approval, that are used to notify off-chain applications about token transfers and approvals.
- **Decentralized Exchanges:** DEXs emit events to signal trades, order book updates, and other relevant events.
- **DAOs:** DAOs use events to record governance proposals, voting results, and other important actions.

Logging

Logging provides a way to record information about the contract's execution for debugging and analysis. It's like leaving notes for yourself or other developers to understand the flow of execution and identify potential issues.

Solidity provides a simple logging mechanism through the console.log function:

Solidity

```
function myFunction() public {
  console.log("This is a log message.");
  // ... other code ...
}
```

This function will print the message "This is a log message" to the console when it's executed. This can be useful for debugging your contract during development.

Important Notes about Logging

- **Development Only:** console.log is mainly used for development and testing purposes. It's not recommended for production contracts, as it adds overhead and can reveal sensitive information.
- **Alternatives for Production:** For production logging, you can use events or other mechanisms to store log data on the blockchain or off-chain storage.

Exercise:

Try adding an event to your SimpleStorage contract from the previous chapter. This event should be emitted whenever the stored value is updated. You can then use Remix's event debugger to capture and view the emitted events.

By understanding events and logging in Solidity, you're gaining valuable tools for making your contracts more transparent, interactive, and debuggable. They allow you to communicate with the outside world, track important events, and gain insights into the inner workings of your contracts.

Chapter 5: Smart Contract Security

Think of smart contract security like building a vault to protect your most precious possessions. You need to consider every possible entry point, reinforce every wall, and anticipate any potential attack vectors. This chapter will guide you through the essential security considerations for Solidity development, helping you build robust and resilient smart contracts that can withstand the test of time (and hackers!).

5.1 Common Vulnerabilities

In the world of smart contracts, these "assets" are often real money or valuable tokens. A single vulnerability can have devastating consequences, potentially leading to financial loss, data breaches, or even the complete shutdown of your decentralized application. So, let's be vigilant and learn how to identify and mitigate these risks!

1. Reentrancy Attacks

Imagine you're withdrawing money from an ATM. You enter the amount, and the machine starts dispensing the cash. But what if, during this process, a cunning thief could somehow trick the machine into dispensing the cash again and again before it updates your account balance? That's essentially what a reentrancy attack does to a smart contract.

In Solidity, a reentrancy attack can occur when a contract calls an external function that then calls back into the original contract before the first function call has completed. This can create a loop where the attacker can repeatedly execute a function, potentially draining funds or manipulating the contract's state.

Example:

Consider a vulnerable withdrawal function in a simple vault contract:

Solidity

```solidity
contract VulnerableVault {
  mapping(address => uint256) public balances;
  function deposit() public payable {
    balances[msg.sender] += msg.value;
  }
  function withdraw(uint256 amount) public {
    require(balances[msg.sender] >= amount, "Insufficient balance.");
    payable(msg.sender).call{value: amount}("");
    balances[msg.sender] -= amount;
  }
}
```

In this code, the contract sends the amount to the user (msg.sender) *before* updating their balance. An attacker could create a malicious contract that, when called by withdraw, calls the withdraw function again within its fallback function. This would create a loop, repeatedly withdrawing funds before the balance is updated, potentially draining the contract.

Mitigation:

- **Checks-Effects-Interactions Pattern:** Structure your functions so that state changes (effects) happen before external calls (interactions). In the example above, update the balance balances[msg.sender] -= amount; *before* sending the Ether payable(msg.sender).call{value: amount}("");.
- **Reentrancy Guards:** Use a modifier or a boolean flag to prevent reentrant calls to a function while it's still

executing. This acts like a lock on the function, preventing it from being called again until the current execution is complete.
- **Pull-over-Push Pattern:** Instead of sending funds directly to the user (push), allow them to "pull" the funds from the contract after the state has been updated. This gives the contract more control over the withdrawal process and prevents reentrancy attacks.

2. Integer Overflow and Underflow

Integers in Solidity have a fixed size (e.g., uint256). When you perform arithmetic operations that result in a value outside the representable range of the integer, an overflow or underflow can occur.

- **Overflow:** Occurs when the result of an addition is larger than the maximum value that the integer can hold. It's like trying to add more water to a glass that's already full – it will spill over.
- **Underflow:** Occurs when the result of a subtraction is smaller than the minimum value that the integer can hold. It's like trying to take more items from a basket than it contains – you can't go below zero.

These can lead to unexpected and potentially harmful behavior in your contract, such as incorrect calculations, unexpected state changes, or even allowing attackers to manipulate the contract's logic.

Example:

Solidity

```
contract IntegerOverflow {

   uint8 public number = 255; // Maximum value for uint8
```

```
function addOne() public {

  number++; // This will overflow to 0

}

}
```

In this example, adding 1 to the maximum value of uint8 (255) will cause it to wrap around to 0. This unexpected behavior could have unintended consequences in your contract's logic.

Mitigation:

- **SafeMath Libraries:** Use SafeMath libraries that provide safe arithmetic operations that check for overflows and underflows before performing calculations. These libraries act like safety nets, preventing your calculations from going out of bounds.
- **Careful Input Validation:** Validate input values to ensure they are within the expected range. This prevents unexpected values from causing overflows or underflows.
- **Solidity Version 0.8.0 and Above:** Solidity versions 0.8.0 and above include built-in overflow and underflow checks by default, making it less likely to encounter these issues. However, it's still good practice to be aware of them and use SafeMath libraries for added safety, especially when dealing with critical calculations.

3. Denial of Service (DoS)

A Denial of Service (DoS) attack aims to make a service or resource unavailable to its legitimate users. In the context of smart contracts, a DoS attack could prevent users from interacting with the contract or cause it to become unresponsive.

Examples of DoS attacks on smart contracts:

- **Gas Limit Attacks:** An attacker could send transactions that consume a lot of gas, making it expensive for other users to interact with the contract.
- **Looping or Recursive Calls:** An attacker could trigger a function that enters an infinite loop or makes recursive calls, consuming all available gas and preventing the contract from executing other transactions.
- **Blocking Operations:** An attacker could send a transaction that blocks the contract's execution, preventing other users from interacting with it.

Mitigation:

- **Rate Limiting:** Implement rate limiting to restrict the number of transactions a user can send within a certain time period.
- **Gas Limits and Fees:** Carefully design your contract's functions and gas costs to prevent attackers from consuming excessive gas.
- **Circuit Breakers:** Implement circuit breaker patterns that halt execution if certain conditions are met, such as excessive gas consumption or repeated failures.

4. Access Control Issues

Access control vulnerabilities occur when unauthorized users can access or modify sensitive functions or data within your contract. This can happen due to:

- **Incorrect Visibility Specifiers:** Using the wrong visibility specifier (e.g., public instead of private) for functions or variables can expose them to unauthorized access.
- **Logic Errors:** Flaws in the contract's logic can allow attackers to bypass access control checks or gain unintended privileges.

- **Missing or Inadequate Authentication:** Failing to properly authenticate users or relying on weak authentication mechanisms can allow attackers to impersonate legitimate users.

Mitigation:

- **Principle of Least Privilege:** Grant only the necessary permissions to users and contracts.
- **Careful Access Control Design:** Use appropriate visibility specifiers and implement robust access control logic.
- **Strong Authentication:** Use strong authentication mechanisms, such as multi-factor authentication or decentralized identity solutions.

By understanding and mitigating these common vulnerabilities, you're taking a significant step towards building more secure smart contracts. In the next section, we'll explore some general security best practices that can further enhance the security of your code.

5.2 Security Best Practices

Think of it like constructing a safe and sturdy building. You wouldn't just start stacking bricks without a plan, right? You'd consider the foundation, the materials, the structural integrity, and potential hazards. Similarly, writing secure smart contracts requires careful planning, attention to detail, and adherence to best practices.

1. Keep it Simple

The more complex your smart contract code, the more likely it is to contain vulnerabilities. It's like building a house with a maze of hidden passages and secret rooms – it becomes much harder to secure and maintain.

Strive for simplicity and clarity in your code. Break down complex logic into smaller, manageable functions. This makes your code easier to understand, audit, and test. Use clear and concise naming conventions for your variables and functions, making it easier to follow the logic and identify potential issues.

Avoid unnecessary complexity or obfuscation. Don't try to be overly clever or use obscure techniques just for the sake of it. Simple and straightforward code is easier to reason about and less likely to contain hidden vulnerabilities.

2. Validate Inputs

Never trust user input! Always validate any data that comes from external sources, such as user input or external contract calls. This helps prevent unexpected or malicious data from affecting your contract's logic. It's like having a security checkpoint at the entrance of your building, checking everyone's ID and ensuring they are authorized to enter.

Use `require` statements to enforce constraints on input values, ensuring that they are within the expected range or meet certain criteria. For example, if your contract expects a positive integer, use a `required` statement to ensure that the input value is not negative or zero.

3. Use SafeMath Libraries

As we discussed in the previous section, integer overflows and underflows can lead to unexpected and potentially harmful behavior in your contracts. To prevent these issues, use SafeMath libraries that provide safe arithmetic operations that check for overflows and underflows before performing calculations.

These libraries act like safety nets, preventing your calculations from going out of bounds and causing unexpected results. They provide functions for basic arithmetic operations like addition, subtraction, multiplication, and division, but with built-in checks to prevent overflows and underflows.

4. Follow the Checks-Effects-Interactions Pattern

Structure your functions to follow the checks-effects-interactions pattern:

- **Checks:** Perform any necessary checks or validations at the beginning of the function. This includes validating inputs, checking balances, or verifying permissions.
- **Effects:** Make any state changes to your contract, such as updating variables or transferring funds.
- **Interactions:** Make any external calls to other contracts or send Ether to external addresses.

This pattern helps prevent reentrancy attacks by ensuring that state changes happen before any external calls. It's like making sure you lock the door before leaving the house, preventing anyone from sneaking in while you're gone.

5. Use Events for Logging and Monitoring

Emit events to log important actions and state changes within your contract. This provides a transparent record of what's happening and allows off-chain applications to monitor the contract's activity. It's like having a security camera that records all activity in your building, providing an audit trail in case something goes wrong.

Events can be used to log things like token transfers, contract updates, or any other significant event that occurs within your contract. This information can be used for debugging, auditing, or providing real-time feedback to users.

6. Protect Your Private Keys

Your private keys are the keys to your kingdom (or at least your contract!). Keep them safe and secure, just like you would protect the keys to your house or your car.

Never hardcode private keys directly in your contract code. This is like leaving your keys under the doormat – anyone who finds them can gain access to your valuables.

Use secure key management techniques, such as:

- **Hardware wallets:** These are physical devices that store your private keys offline, providing an extra layer of security.
- **Multi-signature wallets:** These wallets require multiple parties to authorize a transaction, making it more difficult for attackers to steal funds.

7. Stay Updated

The world of smart contract security is constantly evolving. New vulnerabilities and attack vectors are discovered regularly. Stay informed about the latest security best practices, follow security advisories, and update your contracts to address any known vulnerabilities. It's like keeping your security system up to date with the latest patches and upgrades to protect against new threats.

8. Use a Secure Development Environment

Use a secure development environment and follow secure coding practices. Keep your development tools and libraries up to date. Be mindful of potential security risks when using third-party libraries or integrating with external services. It's like making sure that your construction workers are trustworthy and that the materials you use are free of defects.

9. Consider Formal Verification

For highly critical contracts, consider using formal verification techniques to mathematically prove the correctness and security of your code. This can provide a higher level of assurance, but it can also be complex and time-consuming. It's like having a structural engineer inspect your building to ensure that it meets all safety standards.

Real-world examples:

- **The DAO Hack:** The infamous DAO hack in 2016 exploited a reentrancy vulnerability, resulting in the loss of millions of dollars worth of Ether. This incident highlighted the importance of careful security considerations in smart contract development.
- **Parity Wallet Hacks:** Several vulnerabilities in Parity multi-signature wallets led to significant losses in 2017. These incidents emphasized the need for thorough testing and auditing of smart contracts, especially those that handle large amounts of funds.

By following these security best practices, you can significantly reduce the risk of vulnerabilities in your smart contracts and build more secure and reliable decentralized applications. It's like building a fortress with strong walls, vigilant guards, and a robust security system, protecting your valuable assets from potential threats.

5.3 Testing and Auditing Smart Contracts

Think of testing as putting your contract through a rigorous obstacle course to see if it can withstand various challenges. It's like testing a car's safety features by subjecting it to crash tests and simulations. Auditing, on the other hand, is like having a team of expert mechanics inspect the car's engine and components to identify any potential weaknesses or defects.

Why Testing and Auditing are Essential

Smart contracts, once deployed to the blockchain, become immutable. This means you can't easily fix bugs or vulnerabilities after they're live. It's like launching a rocket into space – once it's gone, you can't easily make changes or repairs. This makes thorough testing and auditing crucial to ensure that your contract is secure and functions as intended before it's released into the wild.

Testing

Testing involves writing automated tests that execute your contract's code and check if it behaves as expected in various scenarios. It's like creating a series of test cases to ensure that your contract can handle different inputs, edge cases, and potential attacks.

Here are some common types of tests for smart contracts:

- **Unit Tests:** These tests focus on individual functions or components of your contract, ensuring that they work correctly in isolation. It's like testing each part of a car individually – the engine, the brakes, the steering – to make sure they function properly.
- **Integration Tests:** These tests check how different parts of your contract interact with each other, ensuring that they work together seamlessly. It's like testing how the car's engine, transmission, and wheels work together to propel the vehicle forward.
- **End-to-End Tests:** These tests simulate real-world usage scenarios, testing the entire flow of your contract from start to finish. It's like taking the car for a test drive on different roads and in different conditions to ensure it performs as expected in real-world situations.
- **Property-Based Tests:** These tests define properties that your contract should satisfy and then generate random

inputs to check if those properties hold true. It's like testing the car's stability by subjecting it to various forces and movements to ensure it doesn't tip over.

Testing Frameworks and Tools

Solidity offers several testing frameworks and tools to help you automate your testing process:

- **Truffle:** Truffle is a popular development environment for Solidity that provides a built-in testing framework. You can write JavaScript tests that interact with your contracts and assert that they behave as expected.
- **Hardhat:** Hard Hat is another popular development environment that includes a testing framework and debugging tools. It offers a more flexible and extensible environment for testing and debugging your contracts.
- **Foundry:** Foundry is a blazing fast testing framework written in Rust. It's known for its speed and efficiency, making it a good choice for large and complex projects.

Writing Effective Tests

Here are some tips for writing effective tests:

- **Test all critical functions:** Make sure to test all the functions that handle sensitive operations or manage valuable assets.
- **Cover edge cases:** Test your contract with edge cases and unexpected inputs to ensure it handles them gracefully.
- **Use assertions:** Use assertions to check that your contract's state and output are as expected after each test case.
- **Automate your tests:** Automate your tests so that they can be run regularly as part of your development process.

Auditing

While testing can catch many common vulnerabilities, it's not a substitute for a professional audit. An audit involves having experienced security experts review your contract's code to identify potential vulnerabilities that automated tests might miss. It's like having a team of expert mechanics inspect your car to identify any potential issues that you might not have noticed.

Auditors will examine your code for common security issues like:

- **Reentrancy:** They will check for potential reentrancy vulnerabilities, where an attacker could repeatedly call a function to drain funds or manipulate the contract's state.
- **Integer Overflows and Underflows:** They will ensure that your code handles integer arithmetic correctly and prevents overflows and underflows that could lead to unexpected behavior.
- **Logic Errors:** They will analyze the logic of your contract to identify potential flaws or inconsistencies that could be exploited by attackers.
- **Access Control:** They will verify that your contract has proper access control mechanisms in place to prevent unauthorized access to sensitive functions or data.

Benefits of Auditing

- **Independent Verification:** Auditors provide an independent and unbiased assessment of your contract's security. They are not involved in the development process, so they can provide an objective perspective.
- **Expert Knowledge:** Auditors have deep expertise in smart contract security and can identify subtle vulnerabilities that might be missed by automated tests or less experienced developers.

- **Increased Confidence:** A successful audit can increase confidence in the security of your contract, reassuring users and investors that their funds and data are safe.

When to Audit

It's generally recommended to have your contracts audited before deploying them to the mainnet, especially if they handle significant value or perform critical functions. This helps ensure that your contract is as secure as possible before it's exposed to real-world users and potential attackers.

Real-world examples:

- **OpenZeppelin:** OpenZeppelin is a popular library of secure and audited smart contracts that can be used as building blocks for your own contracts. They provide implementations of common standards like ERC-20 tokens and access control mechanisms, which have been thoroughly audited and tested.
- **ConsenSys Diligence:** ConsenSys Diligence is a leading smart contract auditing firm that has audited many high-profile projects in the blockchain space. They provide comprehensive audits that identify potential vulnerabilities and offer recommendations for improvements.
- **Trail of Bits:** Trail of Bits is another reputable security firm that provides smart contract auditing services. They use advanced techniques like formal verification to mathematically prove the correctness and security of your code.

Exercise:

Try writing some simple tests for your SimpleStorage contract from Chapter 2. You can use the Truffle testing framework to write JavaScript tests that call the set and get functions and verify that they behave as expected. This will give you a basic understanding of how to write automated tests for your contracts.

By incorporating testing and auditing into your smart contract development process, you can significantly increase the security and reliability of your contracts. This will help you build trust with your users and ensure that your decentralized applications operate safely and effectively in the real world.

Chapter 6: Advanced Solidity

You've mastered the basics of Solidity, and you're ready to level up your smart contract game! In this chapter, we'll explore some more advanced concepts that will allow you to write even more powerful, efficient, and sophisticated contracts. Think of it like progressing from building simple structures to constructing complex architectural marvels. These advanced techniques will expand your toolkit and enable you to create truly innovative decentralized applications.

6.1 Contract Inheritance and Interfaces

Think of inheritance as creating a family tree for your contracts. You can define a parent contract with common properties and functions, and then create child contracts that inherit those properties and functions, adding their own unique characteristics. Interfaces, on the other hand, are like blueprints that specify a set of functions that contracts must implement, ensuring compatibility and interoperability.

Inheritance

Inheritance allows you to create new contracts that inherit properties (variables) and functions from existing contracts. This promotes code reuse and reduces redundancy, as you don't have to rewrite the same code in multiple contracts. It also helps you create a hierarchical structure for your contracts, making them more organized and easier to understand.

How Inheritance Works in Solidity

In Solidity, you use the is keyword to indicate inheritance:

Solidity

```
contract Animal {
```

```
    string public name;
    constructor(string memory _name) {
        name = _name;
    }
    function makeSound() public virtual pure returns (string memory) {
        return "Generic animal sound";
    }
}
contract Dog is Animal {
    function makeSound() public override pure returns (string memory) {
        return "Woof!";
    }
}
```

In this example:

- We define a base contract called Animal with a name variable and a makeSound function.
- The Dog contract inherits from the Animal contract using the is keyword.
- The Dog contract inherits the name variable and the constructor from the Animal contract.
- The Dog contract overrides the makeSound function to provide a dog-specific sound ("Woof!").
- The virtual keyword in the Animal contract allows the makeSound function to be overridden by derived contracts.
- The override keyword in the Dog contract explicitly indicates that the function is overriding a function from the base contract.

Benefits of Inheritance

- **Code Reusability:** Avoid redundant code by inheriting from existing contracts.
- **Modularity:** Create a modular and organized code structure.
- **Extensibility:** Easily extend existing contracts with new functionalities.
- **Polymorphism:** Allow different contracts to implement the same function in different ways (as shown in the makeSound example).

Real-World Examples

- **ERC-20 Token Standards:** Many ERC-20 token contracts inherit from standard ERC-20 interfaces or base contracts, ensuring compatibility and implementing common functionalities.
- **Access Control:** Access control contracts can be inherited to provide common access control mechanisms to different parts of your dApp.
- **Upgradeable Contracts:** Inheritance can be used to create upgradeable contracts, where new versions of a contract inherit from older versions, allowing for bug fixes and feature additions without disrupting existing functionality.

Interfaces

Interfaces define a set of functions that a contract must implement. They are like contracts that only specify function signatures without any implementation. This allows different contracts to adhere to the same interface, ensuring compatibility and interoperability.

Think of it like a standard electrical outlet. Different devices can be plugged into the same outlet because they all conform to the same interface (the shape and configuration of the plug).

Defining and Implementing Interfaces

In Solidity, you use the interface keyword to define an interface:

Solidity

```solidity
interface ERC20 {
  function totalSupply() external view returns (uint256);
  function balanceOf(address account) external view returns (uint256);
  function transfer(address to, uint256 amount) external returns (bool);
  // ... other functions ...
}
contract MyToken is ERC20 {
  // ... implementation of all the functions defined in the ERC20 interface ...
}
```

In this example:

- The ERC20 interface defines the standard functions that an ERC-20 token contract must implement.
- The MyToken contract implements the ERC20 interface by providing concrete implementations for all the functions defined in the interface.

Benefits of Interfaces

- **Standardization:** Promote standardization and interoperability between different contracts.
- **Abstraction:** Abstract away implementation details, allowing for flexibility and modularity.

- **Code Clarity:** Make your code more readable and understandable by clearly defining the expected behaviors.

Real-World Examples

- **ERC-20 and ERC-721 Token Standards:** These widely used token standards are defined as interfaces, ensuring that all tokens that adhere to these standards have a common set of functions.
- **Decentralized Exchanges:** DEXs often use interfaces to interact with different tokens, allowing them to support a wide variety of tokens without needing to know the specific implementation details of each token contract.
- **Oracles:** Oracles, which provide external data to smart contracts, often use interfaces to define how contracts can request and receive data.

Exercise:

1. Try creating a base contract with a few functions, and then create a derived contract that inherits from it and adds some new functionality.
2. Define an interface for a simple game with functions like startGame, makeMove, and endGame. Then, create a contract that implements this interface.

By understanding inheritance and interfaces, you're gaining powerful tools for structuring and organizing your smart contracts. They promote code reuse, modularity, and interoperability, making your dApps more robust, maintainable, and scalable.

6.2 Libraries and Using External Code

Think of libraries like specialized toolkits that provide pre-built functions and functionalities for common tasks. Instead of reinventing the wheel every time you need a specific function, you can simply import a library and use its ready-made tools. This not only saves you time but also allows you to benefit from the expertise of other developers who have already solved common problems and optimized their code for efficiency and security.

What are Libraries in Solidity?

In Solidity, a library is a special type of contract that contains reusable code. Unlike regular contracts, libraries cannot have state variables or receive Ether. They are purely collections of functions that can be called by other contracts.

Why Use Libraries?

Libraries offer several benefits:

- **Modularity:** They help you break down your code into smaller, more manageable modules, making it easier to understand, maintain, and update.
- **Code Reuse:** They allow you to reuse existing code, saving you time and effort. You don't have to write the same functions over and over again.
- **Efficiency:** Libraries can be optimized for gas efficiency, reducing the cost of deploying and interacting with your contracts.
- **Security:** Well-tested and audited libraries can improve the security of your contracts by providing secure implementations of common functionalities.

How to Use Libraries

To use a library in your contract, you first need to import it using the import statement:

Solidity

```
import "./SafeMath.sol";
```

This line imports a library called SafeMath that's located in a file named SafeMath.sol in the same directory as your contract.

Once you've imported the library, you can use its functions in your contract. Here's an example of using the SafeMath library to perform safe addition:

Solidity

```solidity
contract MyContract {

  using SafeMath for uint256;

  function addNumbers(uint256 a, uint256 b) public pure returns (uint256) {

    return a.add(b); // Use the add function from the SafeMath library

  }

}
```

In this example, the using SafeMath for uint256; statement tells the compiler to use the SafeMath library for all uint256 operations within the MyContract contract. This allows you to call the add function from the library directly on uint256 variables, as shown in the a.add(b) expression.

Using External Code

In addition to libraries, you can also use external code from other contracts. This allows you to leverage existing functionalities and build upon the work of others.

Calling External Functions

To call a function from another contract, you need to know its address and function signature. Here's an example:

Solidity

```solidity
contract MyContract {

  function callOtherContract(address otherContractAddress, uint256 value) public {

    // Call the 'myFunction' function on the other contract

    (bool success, bytes memory data) = otherContractAddress.call(abi.encodeWithSignature("myFunction(uint256)", value));

    require(success, "Call failed.");

    // ... process the returned data ...

  }

}
```

In this example, the callOtherContract function calls the myFunction function on another contract at the specified address.

Important Considerations

When using external code, it's important to be aware of potential security risks:

- **Trustworthy Sources:** Only use code from trusted sources. Malicious code could compromise your contract's security.
- **Audits and Reviews:** Look for libraries and contracts that have been audited or reviewed by reputable security experts.

- **Understand the Code:** Make sure you understand how the external code works and its potential implications for your contract's security and functionality.

Real-world examples:

- **OpenZeppelin:** OpenZeppelin is a popular library of secure and audited smart contracts that provide implementations of common standards like ERC-20 tokens, access control mechanisms, and upgradeable contracts.
- **Chainlink:** Chain Link provides a decentralized oracle network that connects smart contracts to real-world data. You can use Chain Link to access data feeds, APIs, and other external resources within your contracts.
- **Uniswap:** Uniswap is a decentralized exchange that provides a library for interacting with its core contracts, allowing developers to build applications that integrate with Uniswap's functionality.

Exercise:

Try using the OpenZeppelin ERC-20 library to create your own custom ERC-20 token contract. This will give you hands-on experience with using external libraries and building upon existing code.

By leveraging libraries and external code, you can accelerate your smart contract development process, improve the quality of your code, and tap into the collective knowledge and expertise of the Solidity community. It's like having a team of experienced developers working alongside you, providing you with the tools and resources you need to build secure and efficient decentralized applications.

6.3 Working with Low-level Calls

Think of low-level calls as the "assembly language" of contract interactions. Just as assembly language gives you direct access to the computer's hardware, low-level calls give you direct access to the underlying mechanisms of how contracts communicate with each other. This can be useful for advanced use cases, but it also requires a deeper understanding of how things work under the hood.

Why Use Low-level Calls?

While Solidity provides high-level functions for interacting with other contracts (like calling a function by name), low-level calls offer more flexibility and control. Here are some reasons why you might use them:

- **Calling Contracts Without Knowing Their Interface:** You can call functions on a contract even if you don't know its interface (the names and signatures of its functions). This can be useful when interacting with legacy contracts or contracts that don't have a well-defined interface.
- **Handling Different Return Types:** Low-level calls allow you to handle different return types more flexibly. You can receive the raw return data from the called contract and process it according to your needs.
- **Implementing Proxy Contracts:** Low-level calls are essential for implementing proxy contracts, which are contracts that forward calls to other contracts. This is a common pattern in upgradeable contracts.

Low-level Call Functions

Solidity provides three main functions for making low-level calls:

- call: This is the most general-purpose low-level call function. It can be used to call any function on another contract, with or without Ether. It returns a boolean value indicating whether the call was successful and a byte array containing the return data from the called contract.

- **delegatecall:** This function is similar to call, but it executes the code of the called contract in the context of the calling contract. This means that the called contract's code can access and modify the storage of the calling contract. This is often used for implementing libraries or upgradeable contracts.
- **staticcall:** This function is similar to call, but it prevents the called contract from modifying the state of the blockchain. This is useful for read-only operations or when you want to ensure that the called contract cannot make any state changes.

Example: Using call

Solidity

```
contract MyContract {

  function callOtherContract(address otherContract, bytes memory data) public {

    // Call the other contract with the provided data

    (bool success, bytes memory returnedData) = otherContract.call(data);

    require(success, "Call failed.");

    // ... process returnedData ...

  }

}
```

In this example, the callOtherContract function takes the address of another contract and a byte array (data) as input. It then uses the call function to call the other contract with the provided data.

The call function returns a boolean value (success) indicating whether the call was successful and a byte array (returnedData) containing the return data from the called contract.

Constructing Call Data

To call a specific function on another contract using low-level calls, you need to construct the call data in the correct format. This involves encoding the function signature and any arguments using the abi.encodeWithSignature function.

For example, to call a function named myFunction(uint256) with the value 123, you would use the following code:

Solidity

```solidity
bytes memory data =
abi.encodeWithSignature("myFunction(uint256)",
123);
```

Important Considerations

When using low-level calls, it's crucial to be aware of potential security risks:

- **Reentrancy Attacks:** Low-level calls can be vulnerable to reentrancy attacks if not handled carefully. Make sure to follow the checks-effects-interactions pattern and use reentrancy guards if necessary.
- **Unexpected Behavior:** The called contract might behave in unexpected ways or have vulnerabilities that could affect your contract. Only call contracts that you trust and understand.
- **Gas Consumption:** Low-level calls can consume a significant amount of gas, especially if the called contract performs complex operations. Be mindful of gas costs and optimize your code accordingly.

Real-world examples:

- **Proxy Contracts:** Proxy contracts often use delegate calls to forward calls to implementation contracts, allowing for upgradeable contracts.
- **Multi-signature Wallets:** Multi-signature wallets might use low-level calls to interact with other contracts on behalf of the wallet's owners.
- **Cross-contract Communication:** Low-level calls can be used for complex cross-contract communication scenarios where high-level function calls might not be sufficient.

Exercise:

Try creating a simple contract that uses delegate calls to call a function in another contract. This will give you a basic understanding of how delegatecall works and how it can be used to share code between contracts.

By understanding low-level calls, you're gaining a deeper understanding of how contracts interact with each other and gaining more control over the interaction process. However, it's crucial to use these powerful tools with caution and be mindful of potential security risks.

6.4 Gas Optimization Techniques

Optimizing your Solidity code for gas efficiency is crucial for several reasons:

- **Reduce Costs:** Lower gas consumption means lower transaction fees for you and your users. This can make your dApp more attractive and accessible to a wider audience.
- **Improve Performance:** Efficient code executes faster, leading to a better user experience.

- **Enhance Scalability:** Gas-efficient contracts can handle more transactions and users without causing network congestion.

So, let's explore some techniques that can help you write learner, meaner, and more gas-efficient Solidity code!

1. Minimize Storage Access:

Accessing storage (reading or writing to the blockchain) is one of the most expensive operations in Solidity. It's like accessing files on a hard drive – it takes time and resources. To minimize gas costs, try to reduce the number of times your contract accesses storage.

Here are some tips:

- **Cache Variables:** If you need to access a storage variable multiple times within a function, read it once and store it in a local memory variable. This avoids repeated storage reads.
- **Update Storage Efficiently:** If you need to update multiple storage variables, try to do it in a single transaction to reduce the number of writes.
- **Use Mappings Efficiently:** When using mappings, try to avoid unnecessary lookups. If you need to check if a key exists in a mapping, use the exists() function instead of directly accessing the mapping.

2. Use Short Data Types:

The size of the data types you use can significantly impact gas consumption. Smaller data types use less storage and require less gas to process.

- **Choose the Right Size:** Use the smallest possible data type that can accommodate your data. For example, if you're storing a small number, use uint8 instead of uint256.

- **Pack Structs:** When defining structs, order the variables from smallest to largest to minimize storage space. This is because Solidity pads variables to 32 bytes, so packing smaller variables together can save space.

3. Avoid Unnecessary Computations

Every computation in your contract consumes gas. Avoid unnecessary calculations or loops, especially within functions that are called frequently.

- **Optimize Loops:** If you're using loops, try to minimize the number of iterations and the amount of work done within each iteration.
- **Pre-calculate Values:** If you can pre-calculate a value instead of calculating it repeatedly, do so.
- **Use Libraries:** Libraries can be optimized for gas efficiency, so consider using them for common operations.

4. Use Modifiers Efficiently

Modifiers can help you avoid repeating code, which can reduce code size and gas costs. If you have a common check or condition that needs to be applied to multiple functions, use a modifier instead of repeating the code in each function.

5. Optimize Function Visibility: Public vs. Private

Public functions are more expensive to call than private or internal functions. If a function is only called internally within your contract, make it private or internal to reduce gas costs.

6. Use Events Judiciously

While events are useful for logging and communication, emitting too many events can increase gas costs. Only emit events for truly important actions or state changes.

7. Use Assembly When Necessary

For highly performance-critical operations, you can use inline assembly to write low-level code that interacts directly with the EVM. This can give you more fine-grained control over gas usage, but it also requires a deeper understanding of the EVM's architecture and can make your code harder to read and maintain.

Real-world examples:

- **GasToken:** GasToken is a token that allows users to "store" gas when prices are low and "release" it when prices are high, effectively hedging against gas price fluctuations.
- **Optimized DeFi Protocols:** Decentralized finance (DeFi) protocols often employ gas optimization techniques to minimize transaction fees for users, making their platforms more competitive.
- **NFT Minting:** Efficient NFT minting contracts can reduce the gas cost of creating new NFTs, making them more accessible to a wider audience.

Exercise:

Take a look at the SimpleStorage contract from Chapter 2 and try to optimize it for gas usage. Can you reduce the gas cost of the set and get functions?

By applying these gas optimization techniques, you can significantly reduce the cost of deploying and interacting with your smart contracts. This will make your dApps more efficient, scalable, and user-friendly, contributing to a better overall experience for your users.

Chapter 7: ERC-20 Tokens

It's time to create your own cryptocurrency! In this chapter, we'll explore the world of ERC-20 tokens, the most popular standard for creating fungible tokens on the Ethereum blockchain. Think of ERC-20 tokens as the digital equivalent of cash – they're interchangeable, divisible, and can be used for a wide variety of purposes, from representing value to governing decentralized organizations.

We'll start by understanding the ERC-20 standard, then walk through the process of creating your own token, and finally explore the core functionalities that make these tokens so versatile.

7.1 Understanding the ERC-20 Standard

Let's dive into the world of ERC-20 tokens! This is the most widely used standard for creating fungible tokens on the Ethereum blockchain. Think of it as the blueprint for building digital assets that can represent anything from a virtual currency to a share in a company, a loyalty point, or even a voting right in a decentralized organization.

What Exactly *is* an ERC-20 Token?

Before we get into the nitty-gritty of the standard, let's clarify what we mean by "fungible." Fungibility means that every unit of a token is interchangeable with any other unit. Just like a dollar bill is the same as any other dollar bill, one ERC-20 token is identical to any other token of the same type. This makes them perfect for representing things that need to be easily exchanged or traded.

The ERC-20 standard itself is a set of rules and guidelines that define how these tokens should behave on the Ethereum blockchain. It ensures that different tokens can interact seamlessly with each other and with various applications and wallets. Think of it like the standard dimensions for a credit card – all credit cards follow the same basic size and shape so they can be used in any ATM or card reader. Similarly, the ERC-20 standard provides a common framework for token creation, ensuring compatibility and interoperability within the Ethereum ecosystem.

Key Components of the ERC-20 Standard

The ERC-20 standard outlines several key components that every compliant token contract must implement:

1. **Token Information:** This includes basic information about the token, such as:
    - name: The human-readable name of the token (e.g., "My Awesome Token").
    - symbol: A short abbreviation for the token (e.g., "MAT").
    - decimals: The number of decimal places the token uses (e.g., 18 for most tokens).
    - totalSupply: The total number of tokens in existence.
2. **Account Balances:** The standard specifies how to keep track of the balances of token holders. This is typically done using a mapping data structure that maps Ethereum addresses to their corresponding token balances.
3. **Transfer Function** (transfer)**:** This function allows users to transfer tokens to other addresses. It takes two arguments: the recipient's address and the amount of tokens to transfer.
4. **Approval Function** (approve)**:** This function allows users to authorize another address (a "spender") to spend a certain amount of their tokens on their behalf. This is useful for scenarios like decentralized exchanges, where users need to allow the exchange contract to spend their tokens to facilitate trades.
5. **Transfer From Function** (transferFrom)**:** This function allows a spender (who has been previously approved) to

transfer tokens from another account, up to the approved amount.
6. **Events:** The standard defines events that are emitted when certain actions occur, such as token transfers or approvals. These events provide a transparent record of token activity and can be used by off-chain applications to monitor and react to token movements.

Benefits of Using the ERC-20 Standard

- **Interoperability:** ERC-20 tokens can be easily integrated with other ERC-20 tokens and applications. This means you can use your token with various wallets, exchanges, and dApps without any compatibility issues.
- **Standardization:** The standard ensures that all ERC-20 tokens have a common set of functionalities, making them easier to use and understand. This reduces the learning curve for developers and users alike.
- **Wide Adoption:** The ERC-20 standard is widely adopted in the Ethereum ecosystem, making it the most popular choice for creating fungible tokens. This means there's a large community of developers and users familiar with the standard, providing ample support and resources.
- **Security:** By adhering to the ERC-20 standard and using well-tested implementations, you can reduce the risk of security vulnerabilities in your token contract.

Real-world examples:

- **DAI:** DAI is a stablecoin that uses the ERC-20 standard. It's designed to maintain a stable value pegged to the US dollar, providing a safe haven for cryptocurrency investors during market volatility.
- **USDC:** USDC is another popular stablecoin that follows the ERC-20 standard. It's backed by US dollar reserves and is widely used for trading and payments in the crypto space.

- **LINK:** LINK is the native token of the Chainlink decentralized oracle network. It's used to pay node operators for providing real-world data to smart contracts.
- **UNI:** UNI is the governance token of the Uniswap decentralized exchange. It allows holders to participate in the governance of the protocol and vote on proposals.

Exercise:

Research some popular ERC-20 tokens and explore their functionalities. Look at their contract code (available on Etherscan) and identify the key components of the ERC-20 standard that they implement.

By understanding the ERC-20 standard, you're gaining a solid foundation for creating your own tokens and participating in the vibrant world of decentralized finance and Web3 applications. It's a powerful standard that has enabled the creation of countless tokens and fueled the growth of the Ethereum ecosystem.

7.2 Creating Your Own Token

It's time to roll up our sleeves and create your very own ERC-20 token! This is where you'll put your Solidity skills to the test and bring your token idea to life on the Ethereum blockchain. Think of it as minting your own digital currency, with its own unique name, symbol, and purpose.

Steps to Create an ERC-20 Token

Creating an ERC-20 token involves writing a Solidity smart contract that adheres to the ERC-20 standard. Here's a step-by-step guide:

1. **Define Token Information:** Start by defining the basic information about your token. This includes:

- **Name:** The human-readable name of your token (e.g., "AwesomeToken").
- **Symbol:** A short abbreviation for your token (e.g., "AWT").
- **Decimals:** The number of decimal places your token uses. Most tokens use 18 decimals, which allows for fractional ownership.
- **Total Supply:** The total number of tokens that will ever exist.

2. **Implement the ERC-20 Functions:** The core of your token contract is the implementation of the standard ERC-20 functions. These functions define how users can interact with your token, such as transferring tokens, approving spending, and checking balances.
3. **Here are the essential ERC-20 functions:**
    - totalSupply(): Returns the total supply of tokens.
    - balanceOf(address account): Returns the token balance of a given address.
    - transfer(address to, uint256 amount): Transfers tokens from the sender's account to another address.
    - allowance(address owner, address spender): Returns the remaining number of tokens that a spender is allowed to spend on behalf of an owner.
    - approve(address spender, uint256 amount): Allows an owner to authorize a spender to spend a certain amount of their tokens.
    - transferFrom(address from, address to, uint256 amount): Allows a spender to transfer tokens from an owner's account to another address, up to the approved amount.
4. **Emit Events:** Emit the necessary ERC-20 events to provide a transparent record of token activity. The two main events are:

- Transfer(address indexed from, address indexed to, uint256 value): Emitted whenever tokens are transferred.
- Approval(address indexed owner, address indexed spender, uint256 value): Emitted whenever a spender is approved to spend tokens on behalf of an owner.

Example Code: Creating a Simple ERC-20 Token

Solidity

```
pragma solidity ^0.8.0;

import "@openzeppelin/contracts/token/ERC20/ERC20.sol";

contract MyToken is ERC20 {

    constructor() ERC20("MyToken", "MTK") {

        _mint(msg.sender, 1000000 [1] * 10 ** 18);

    }

}
```

In this example:

- We use the pragma solidity ^0.8.0; directive to specify the Solidity compiler version.
- We import the ERC20.sol contract from the OpenZeppelin library. This provides a secure and audited implementation of the ERC-20 standard, saving us from having to write all the code from scratch.
- We define our token contract, MyToken, which inherits from the ERC20 contract.

- In the constructor, we call the ERC20 constructor to initialize the token with a name ("MyToken"), symbol ("MTK"), and then mint an initial supply of 1 million tokens (multiplied by 10^18 to account for 18 decimals) to the contract deployer (msg.sender).

Using OpenZeppelin

The OpenZeppelin library is a valuable resource for Solidity developers. It provides secure and audited implementations of common smart contract standards and functionalities, including ERC-20 tokens. Using OpenZeppelin can save you time and effort and help you avoid common security vulnerabilities.

Compiling and Deploying Your Token

Once you've written your token contract, you can compile and deploy it using your preferred development environment (Remix, Hardhat, Truffle, etc.). Make sure to deploy it to a testnet first to experiment and test its functionality before deploying it to the mainnet.

Real-World Examples

Countless tokens have been created using the ERC-20 standard, powering a wide range of applications and use cases:

- **Stablecoins:** Tokens like DAI and USDC are pegged to the value of stable assets like the US dollar, providing stability and reducing volatility in the crypto market.
- **Governance Tokens:** Tokens like UNI (Uniswap) and AAVE (Aave) are used for governance in decentralized organizations, allowing token holders to vote on proposals and participate in decision-making.
- **Utility Tokens:** Many dApps have their own utility tokens that are used to access services, pay for transactions, or incentivize participation within the platform.

Exercise:

Try modifying the example code above to:

- Change the token name, symbol, and total supply.
- Add a function to burn tokens (reduce the total supply).
- Add a function to mint new tokens (increase the total supply), but restrict it so that only the contract owner can call it.

By creating your own ERC-20 token, you're not only gaining valuable experience in Solidity development but also contributing to the growing world of decentralized finance and Web3 applications. Your token could be the next big thing in the crypto space!

7.3 Token Functionality (Transfer, Approve, etc.)

Let's explore the core functionalities that make ERC-20 tokens so versatile and powerful! These functions define how users can interact with your token, enabling actions like transferring tokens between accounts, approving spending, and checking balances. Think of these functions as the buttons and levers that control your token's behavior, allowing users to participate in the token economy you've created.

1. transfer

The transfer function is the most fundamental operation in an ERC-20 token. It allows a token holder to transfer a specified amount of tokens to another address. It's like sending money from your bank account to someone else's account.

the function signature:

Solidity

```solidity
function transfer(address to, uint256 amount)
public returns (bool);
```

- to: The address of the recipient.
- amount: The amount of tokens to transfer.
- returns (bool): The function returns a boolean value indicating whether the transfer was successful.

Example Usage:

Solidity

```solidity
// Transfer 100 tokens to another address

myToken.transfer(anotherAddress, 100 * 10 ** 18);
```

In this example, myToken is an instance of your ERC-20 token contract, anotherAddress is the recipient's address, and 100 * 10 ** 18 represents 100 tokens (multiplied by 10^18 to account for decimals).

2. approve

The approve function allows a token holder to authorize another address (a "spender") to spend a certain amount of their tokens on their behalf. This is useful for scenarios like decentralized exchanges, where users need to allow the exchange contract to spend their tokens to facilitate trades.

Here's the function signature:

Solidity

```solidity
function approve(address spender, uint256 amount)
public returns (bool);
```

- **spender**: The address of the spender who is being authorized.
- **amount**: The amount of tokens that the spender is allowed to spend.
- **returns (bool)**: The function returns a boolean value indicating whether the approval was successful.

Example Usage:

Solidity

```
// Approve another address to spend 500 tokens

myToken.approve(spenderAddress, 500 * 10 ** 18);
```

3. transferFrom

The transferFrom function allows a spender (who has been previously approved) to transfer tokens from an owner's account to another address, up to the approved amount. This function is typically used by decentralized exchanges or other applications that need to facilitate token transfers on behalf of users.

Here's the function signature:

Solidity

```
function transferFrom(address from, address to, uint256 amount) public returns (bool);
```

- **from**: The address of the token owner.
- **to**: The address of the recipient.
- **amount**: The amount of tokens to transfer.
- **returns (bool)**: The function returns a boolean value indicating whether the transfer was successful.

Example Usage:

Solidity

```solidity
// Spender transfers 200 tokens from the owner's account

myToken.transferFrom(ownerAddress, anotherAddress, 200 * 10 ** 18);
```

4. balanceOf

The balanceOf function allows you to check the token balance of a given address. It's like checking your account balance at an ATM.

Here's the function signature:

Solidity

```solidity
function balanceOf(address account) public view returns (uint256);
```

- account: The address of the account whose balance you want to check.
- returns (uint256): The function returns the token balance of the given address.

Example Usage:

Solidity

```solidity
// Get the token balance of an address

uint256 balance = myToken.balanceOf(myAddress);
```

5. allowance

The allowance function allows you to check the remaining number of tokens that a spender is allowed to spend on behalf of an owner.

It's like checking how much credit you've given someone on your credit card.

Here's the function signature:

Solidity

```solidity
function allowance(address owner, address spender) public view returns (uint256);
```

- owner: The address of the token owner.
- spender: The address of the spender.
- returns (uint256): The function returns the remaining number of tokens that the spender is allowed to spend on behalf of the owner.

Example Usage:

Solidity

```solidity
// Get the remaining allowance for a spender

uint256 remainingAllowance = myToken.allowance(ownerAddress, spenderAddress);
```

Real-world examples:

- **Decentralized Exchanges (DEXs):** DEXs like Uniswap and SushiSwap use the approve and transferFrom functions to facilitate token swaps between users. Users approve the DEX contract to spend their tokens, and the DEX then uses transferFrom to transfer tokens between the users involved in the trade.
- **Yield Farming:** In yield farming, users deposit their tokens into smart contracts to earn rewards. These contracts often use the transferFrom function to move tokens between different accounts as users deposit, withdraw, or claim rewards.

- **NFT Marketplaces:** NFT marketplaces like OpenSea use the transferFrom function to transfer ownership of NFTs from sellers to buyers.

Exercise:

Try interacting with a popular ERC-20 token contract using a tool like Remix or a Web3 library like Web3.js. Experiment with the transfer, approve, and transferFrom functions to understand how they work in practice.

By understanding these core ERC-20 token functionalities, you're gaining the knowledge to build powerful and versatile decentralized applications that can handle a wide range of token-based interactions. These functions are the building blocks of the token economy, enabling users to transfer, spend, and manage their digital assets in a secure and decentralized manner.

Chapter 8: NFTs (Non-Fungible Tokens)

Let's dive into the exciting world of NFTs! You've probably heard about them – those unique digital assets that have taken the art, gaming, and collectibles worlds by storm. But what exactly are they, and how do they work? In this chapter, we'll explore the fascinating world of Non-Fungible Tokens (NFTs), learn about the ERC-721 standard that governs them, and discover how to create and manage your own NFTs using Solidity.

8.1 What are NFTs?

You've probably heard the term thrown around a lot lately, associated with digital art, collectibles, and even virtual real estate. But what exactly *are* these Non-Fungible Tokens, and why are they causing such a stir?

NFTs

At their core, NFTs are unique digital assets that represent ownership of a specific item or piece of content. They're like digital collectibles, each with its own distinct identity and value. Unlike cryptocurrencies like Bitcoin or Ether, which are fungible (meaning one unit is interchangeable with another), NFTs are non-fungible. This means that each NFT is unique and cannot be replaced by another token.

Think of it like this: a dollar bill is fungible because any dollar bill can be exchanged for any other dollar bill. They all have the same value and are interchangeable. But a rare trading card or a one-of-a-kind painting is non-fungible because it's unique and cannot be replaced by another card or painting, even if they look similar.

How NFTs Work

NFTs leverage blockchain technology to establish verifiable ownership and provenance of digital assets. This means that the ownership history of an NFT is permanently recorded on the blockchain, making it transparent and tamper-proof.

Here's a simplified breakdown of how it works:

1. **Creation:** An NFT is created (or "minted") on a blockchain, typically Ethereum. This involves creating a unique token ID and associating it with a specific digital asset, such as an image, video, or piece of text.
2. **Ownership:** The NFT represents ownership of that digital asset. The owner's address is recorded on the blockchain, and they can prove their ownership using their private key.
3. **Transfer:** NFTs can be transferred or sold to other users. This transfer is recorded on the blockchain, creating a transparent and auditable history of ownership.
4. **Verification:** Anyone can verify the authenticity and ownership of an NFT by looking up its information on the blockchain.

Key Characteristics of NFTs

- **Uniqueness:** Each NFT is unique and distinct from all other NFTs. This is ensured by the unique token ID assigned to each NFT.
- **Indivisibility:** NFTs cannot be divided into smaller units. You can't own a fraction of an NFT, just like you can't own half a painting.
- **Ownership:** NFTs represent ownership of a specific asset or piece of content. This ownership is verifiable and secure thanks to blockchain technology.

- **Transferability:** NFTs can be transferred or sold to other users. This transfer is recorded on the blockchain, creating a transparent and auditable history of ownership.
- **Authenticity:** Blockchain technology ensures the authenticity and provenance of NFTs. This means that you can be sure that an NFT is genuine and that its ownership history is accurate.

Real-World Examples of NFTs

- **Digital Art:** NFTs have revolutionized the art world by allowing artists to create and sell unique digital artwork. Platforms like SuperRare and Foundation enable artists to tokenize their creations and sell them directly to collectors.
- **Collectibles:** NFTs are used to represent digital collectibles, such as trading cards, virtual pets, and in-game items. These collectibles can be bought, sold, and traded on various marketplaces.
- **Gaming:** NFTs are transforming the gaming industry by giving players true ownership of in-game assets. This allows players to buy, sell, and trade items, characters, and even virtual land within games.
- **Music:** Musicians are using NFTs to release and sell their music directly to fans, bypassing traditional record labels and distribution channels.
- **Metaverses:** NFTs are used to represent ownership of virtual land, avatars, and other assets in metaverses, creating immersive and interactive virtual worlds.
- **Event Tickets:** NFTs can be used to create unique and verifiable tickets for events, preventing fraud and scalping.
- **Physical Assets:** NFTs can be used to represent ownership of physical assets, such as real estate, cars, or even luxury goods. This can streamline the process of buying and selling these assets and provide a secure record of ownership.

Exercise:

Explore some popular NFT marketplaces like OpenSea, Rarible, or SuperRare. Browse through the different collections and see the variety of NFTs available. Choose an NFT that interests you and examine its properties and ownership history on the blockchain.

By understanding the concepts and applications of NFTs, you're opening up a world of possibilities for building innovative and impactful decentralized applications. NFTs are transforming how we think about digital ownership, creativity, and value exchange, and they are poised to play a significant role in the future of the internet.

8.2 The ERC-721 Standard

Just like the ERC-20 standard provides a common framework for fungible tokens, ERC-721 sets the rules for non-fungible tokens. It defines a set of functions and events that all NFT contracts should implement, ensuring consistency and interoperability across the Ethereum ecosystem.

Key Components of the ERC-721 Standard

The ERC-721 standard outlines several key components that every compliant NFT contract must have:

1. **Token Metadata:** This includes information about the NFT, such as:
   - name**:** The name of the NFT collection (e.g., "My Awesome NFTs").
   - symbol**:** A short abbreviation for the collection (e.g., "MAN").
   - tokenURI(uint256 tokenId)**:** A function that returns a Uniform Resource Identifier (URI) pointing to the metadata of a specific NFT. This metadata typically

includes information like the NFT's name, description, image, and other attributes.
2. **Ownership:** The standard specifies how to keep track of who owns each NFT. This is typically done using a mapping that maps each unique token ID (uint256) to the address of its owner.
3. **Transfer Functions:** These functions allow users to transfer NFTs between addresses:
    - safeTransferFrom(address from, address to, uint256 tokenId): This function transfers an NFT from one address to another, ensuring that the recipient is capable of handling the NFT (e.g., it's not a contract that doesn't support ERC-721).
    - transferFrom(address from, address to, uint256 tokenId): This function is similar to safeTransferFrom, but it doesn't perform checks on the recipient, so it should be used with caution.
4. **Approval Functions:** These functions allow users to authorize other addresses to transfer their NFTs on their behalf:
    - approve(address to, uint256 tokenId): This function approves another address to transfer a specific NFT.
    - setApprovalForAll(address operator, bool approved): This function approves or disapproves an operator to transfer all NFTs owned by the caller.
5. **Events:** The standard defines events that are emitted when certain actions occur, such as token transfers or approvals. These events provide a transparent record of NFT activity and can be used by off-chain applications to monitor and react to NFT-related events.
    - Transfer(address indexed from, address indexed to, uint256 indexed tokenId): Emitted whenever an NFT is transferred.

- Approval(address indexed owner, address indexed approved, uint256 indexed tokenId): Emitted whenever an address is approved to transfer an NFT.
- ApprovalForAll(address indexed owner, address indexed operator, bool approved): Emitted whenever an operator is approved or disapproved to transfer all NFTs of an owner.

Benefits of Using the ERC-721 Standard

- **Interoperability:** ERC-721 tokens can be easily integrated with other ERC-721 tokens and applications, such as wallets, marketplaces, and games.
- **Standardization:** The standard ensures that all ERC-721 tokens have a common set of functionalities, making them easier to use and understand.
- **Wide Adoption:** The ERC-721 standard is widely adopted in the Ethereum ecosystem, making it the most popular choice for creating NFTs.
- **Security:** By adhering to the ERC-721 standard and using well-tested implementations, you can reduce the risk of security vulnerabilities in your NFT contract.

Real-World Examples

- **CryptoPunks:** One of the earliest and most successful NFT projects, CryptoPunks are a collection of 10,000 unique pixel art characters that were launched in 2017. Each CryptoPunk is a unique ERC-721 token.
- **Bored Ape Yacht Club:** A collection of 10,000 unique Bored Ape NFTs that grant access to an exclusive online community and various benefits. Bored Ape Yacht Club NFTs have become highly sought-after collectibles in the NFT space.
- **Decentraland:** A decentralized virtual world where users can buy and sell virtual land represented as NFTs. Users can

build structures, create experiences, and interact with each other in this virtual world.

Exercise:

Explore the OpenZeppelin ERC-721 implementation and familiarize yourself with its code. Try creating a simple NFT contract that inherits from the OpenZeppelin ERC721 contract and implements the mint function to create new NFTs.

By understanding the ERC-721 standard, you're gaining a solid foundation for creating your own NFTs and participating in the exciting world of digital ownership and decentralized applications. It's a powerful standard that has enabled the creation of countless unique and valuable digital assets, and it continues to drive innovation in the blockchain space.

8.3 Creating and Managing NFTs

Let's get hands-on and create your own NFTs! This is where you'll combine your Solidity skills with your creative vision to bring unique digital assets to life on the Ethereum blockchain. Think of it as crafting your own digital masterpieces, each with its own distinct identity and story to tell.

Building Your NFT Contract

Creating an NFT involves writing a Solidity smart contract that adheres to the ERC-721 standard. This contract will define the rules and functionalities for your NFTs, such as how they are created, transferred, and managed.

Leveraging OpenZeppelin

To simplify the process and ensure security, we'll use the OpenZeppelin ERC-721 implementation as a foundation for our contract. OpenZeppelin provides a well-tested and audited implementation of the ERC-721 standard, saving you from writing all the code from scratch and reducing the risk of vulnerabilities.

Example Code: A Simple NFT Contract

Solidity

```
pragma solidity ^0.8.0;

import "@openzeppelin/contracts/token/ERC721/ERC721.sol";

contract MyNFT is ERC721 {

  constructor() ERC721("MyNFT", "MNFT") {}

  function mint(address to, uint256 tokenId) public {

    _mint(to, tokenId); ¹

  }

}
```

Let's break down this code:

- pragma solidity ^0.8.0;: This line specifies the Solidity compiler version to use.
- import "@openzeppelin/contracts/token/ERC721/ERC721.sol";: This line imports the OpenZeppelin ERC721 contract, which provides the implementation of the ERC-721 standard.
- contract MyNFT is ERC721 { ... }: This defines your NFT contract, named MyNFT, which inherits from the OpenZeppelin ERC721 contract.

- constructor() ERC721("MyNFT", "MNFT") {}: This is the constructor of your contract. It calls the ERC721 constructor to initialize your NFT collection with a name ("MyNFT") and a symbol ("MNFT").
- function mint(address to, uint256 tokenId) public { ... }: This function, named mint, allows you to create new NFTs. It takes two arguments:
    - to: The address of the recipient who will own the newly minted NFT.
    - tokenId: A unique identifier for the NFT. This should be a uint256 value that is different for each NFT you create.
    - Inside the function, _mint(to, tokenId); calls the internal _mint function inherited from the ERC721 contract to create the new NFT and assign it to the specified address.

Minting Your First NFT

Once you've deployed this contract to the blockchain (using Remix, Hardhat, or another tool), you can call the mint function to create your first NFT. For example, to mint an NFT with tokenId 1 to the address 0x123..., you would call the function like this:

Solidity

```
myNFT.mint(0x123..., 1);
```

This will create a new NFT with the specified tokenId and assign ownership to the provided address.

Managing Your NFTs

The ERC-721 standard provides several other functions that you can use to manage your NFTs:

- transferFrom(address from, address to, uint256 tokenId): This function allows you to transfer an NFT from one address to another.
- approve(address to, uint256 tokenId): This function allows you to authorize another address to transfer a specific NFT on your behalf.
- setApprovalForAll(address operator, bool approved): This function allows you to approve or disapprove an operator to transfer all of your NFTs.
- balanceOf(address owner): This function returns the number of NFTs owned by a given address.
- ownerOf(uint256 tokenId): This function returns the owner of a specific NFT.

Adding Metadata

The tokenURI function is crucial for associating metadata with your NFTs. This metadata can include information like the NFT's name, description, image, and other attributes. This metadata is typically stored off-chain (e.g., on IPFS) to avoid bloating the blockchain with large files. The tokenURI function returns a URI that points to this metadata.

Real-World Examples

- **CryptoKitties:** One of the earliest and most popular NFT projects, CryptoKitties allows users to breed and trade unique digital cats. Each cat is represented by an ERC-721 token, and its appearance and attributes are determined by its genes, which are stored as metadata.
- **Decentraland:** Decentraland is a decentralized virtual world where users can buy and sell virtual land represented as NFTs. The metadata for each land parcel includes its coordinates, size, and any structures or objects built on it.
- **Axie Infinity:** Axie Infinity is a blockchain-based game where players collect and battle creatures called Axies. Each Axie is an NFT with unique characteristics and abilities, and

its metadata includes its visual appearance, stats, and battle history.

Exercise:

1. Try modifying the example code above to include a tokenURI function that returns a URI for your NFT metadata. You can store this metadata in a JSON file and host it on a service like IPFS.
2. Explore the OpenZeppelin ERC-721 documentation and learn about other functions and features that you can use to manage your NFTs.

By understanding how to create and manage NFTs, you're gaining the power to create unique and valuable digital assets that can be used in a wide range of applications. This is an exciting and rapidly evolving field, and your creativity is the limit!

8.4 NFT Use Cases

Think of NFTs as versatile building blocks that can be used to create a wide range of applications. They're like digital Legos that can be assembled in countless ways to build unique and innovative structures. In this section, we'll explore some of the most promising and impactful use cases for NFTs.

1. Digital Art and Collectibles

NFTs have revolutionized the art world by providing a way for artists to create and sell unique digital artwork. Before NFTs, it was difficult to establish ownership and provenance of digital art because digital files can be easily copied and shared. NFTs solve this problem by providing a secure and verifiable way to represent ownership of digital creations.

How it works:

- Artists can "mint" their artwork as NFTs, creating a unique token that represents ownership of that specific piece.
- Collectors can buy and sell these NFTs on marketplaces like OpenSea, Rarible, and SuperRare.
- The ownership history of the NFT is recorded on the blockchain, providing proof of authenticity and provenance.

Benefits:

- **Artists can monetize their work directly:** NFTs allow artists to bypass traditional intermediaries like galleries and auction houses, connecting directly with collectors and receiving a larger share of the revenue.
- **Collectors can own unique digital assets:** NFTs provide a way for collectors to own verifiable and authentic digital art, just like they would own a physical painting or sculpture.
- **New markets and opportunities:** NFTs have created new markets and opportunities for artists and collectors, expanding the art world beyond the physical realm.

Real-world examples:

- **Beeple's "Everydays: The First 5000 Days":** This digital artwork sold for a record-breaking $69 million at Christie's auction house, highlighting the growing value and recognition of NFT art.
- **CryptoPunks:** One of the earliest and most successful NFT projects, CryptoPunks are a collection of 10,000 unique pixel art characters that have become highly sought-after collectibles.

2. Gaming

NFTs are transforming the gaming industry by giving players true ownership of in-game assets. This means that players can buy, sell, and trade items, characters, and even virtual land within games, creating new economies and opportunities for players and developers.

How it works:

- In-game items and assets are represented as NFTs, giving players verifiable ownership.
- Players can trade these NFTs on marketplaces or exchange them with other players.
- NFTs can be used to create unique in-game experiences, such as access to exclusive content or special abilities.

Benefits:

- **Player ownership and control:** NFTs empower players by giving them true ownership of their in-game assets.
- **New revenue streams:** NFTs create new revenue streams for game developers and players alike.
- **Interoperability:** NFTs can be used across different games, creating a more interconnected gaming ecosystem.

Real-world examples:

- **Axie Infinity:** This blockchain-based game allows players to collect, breed, and battle creatures called Axies. Each Axie is an NFT with unique characteristics and value.
- **Decentraland:** This decentralized virtual world allows users to buy and sell virtual land represented as NFTs. Users can build structures, create experiences, and interact with each other in this virtual world.

3. Metaverses

NFTs are essential building blocks for metaverses, which are immersive and interactive virtual worlds where users can socialize, play games, work, and create. NFTs can represent ownership of virtual land, avatars, and other assets within these metaverses.

How it works:

- Virtual land, avatars, and other assets are represented as NFTs, providing verifiable ownership and scarcity.
- Users can buy, sell, and trade these NFTs, creating a virtual economy within the metaverse.
- NFTs can be used to access exclusive areas, events, or experiences within the metaverse.

Benefits:

- **True ownership in virtual worlds:** NFTs give users true ownership of their virtual assets, creating a sense of ownership and investment in the metaverse.
- **Interoperability:** NFTs can be used across different metaverses, allowing users to take their assets with them between different virtual worlds.
- **New economic opportunities:** Metaverses powered by NFTs create new economic opportunities for creators, developers, and users.

Real-world examples:

- **The Sandbox:** This decentralized gaming platform allows users to create and monetize their own games and experiences within a virtual world.
- **Decentraland:** This virtual world allows users to buy and sell virtual land, build structures, and create experiences.

4. Other Use Cases

The applications of NFTs extend beyond the digital realm. Here are some other exciting use cases:

- **Supply Chain Management:** NFTs can be used to track the provenance and authenticity of physical goods, reducing counterfeiting and improving supply chain transparency. For example, a luxury brand could use NFTs to verify the authenticity of its products.

- **Identity and Access Management:** NFTs can be used to represent digital identities and provide access control to physical or digital resources. For example, an NFT could represent your membership to a gym or your access pass to a concert.
- **Ticketing and Events:** NFTs can be used to create unique and verifiable tickets for events, preventing fraud and scalping. This can also provide new ways for event organizers to engage with attendees and offer exclusive experiences.
- **Real Estate:** NFTs can be used to represent ownership of real estate, streamlining the process of buying and selling property and providing a secure and transparent record of ownership.
- **Intellectual Property:** NFTs can be used to protect and manage intellectual property rights, such as patents, trademarks, and copyrights.

Exercise:

Think about a potential use case for NFTs in your own field or area of interest. How could NFTs be used to represent ownership, create new experiences, or solve existing problems?

By understanding the diverse applications of NFTs, you can start to see their potential to transform various industries and create new opportunities for innovation and value creation. NFTs are not just a fad – they are a powerful technology that is here to stay, and they are poised to play a significant role in the future of the internet and beyond.

Chapter 9: Decentralized Autonomous Organizations (DAOs)

In this chapter, we'll demystify the concept of DAOs, learn how to build a basic DAO using Solidity, explore different governance and voting mechanisms, and discuss crucial security considerations to keep your DAO safe and thriving.

9.1 Understanding DAO Concepts

Think of a DAO as an internet-native community with shared goals, operating transparently and autonomously on a blockchain. It's like a self-governing online community where the rules are set in code, and decisions are made collectively by the members.

What Exactly is a DAO?

A DAO, or Decentralized Autonomous Organization, is essentially an organization that is governed by rules encoded as computer programs called smart contracts. These smart contracts live on a blockchain, which provides a transparent and secure platform for the DAO to operate.

Instead of relying on traditional hierarchical structures with a central authority making decisions, DAOs distribute power among their members. Decisions are made collectively through voting or other consensus mechanisms, ensuring that the organization operates in a democratic and transparent manner.

Key Characteristics of DAOs

Here are some key features that define a DAO:

- **Decentralization:** There is no central authority or single point of control. Power is distributed among the DAO's

members. This makes DAOs resistant to censorship and single points of failure.
- **Autonomy:** DAOs operate independently, based on the rules encoded in their smart contracts. Once deployed, these contracts execute automatically and autonomously, without the need for human intervention.
- **Transparency:** All transactions and decisions within a DAO are recorded on the blockchain, making them publicly auditable and verifiable. This transparency fosters trust and accountability among members.
- **Automation:** Many DAO operations are automated through smart contracts, reducing the need for manual intervention and human error. This can streamline processes and improve efficiency.
- **Community-Driven:** DAOs are typically governed by their communities, with members having a say in the organization's direction and decisions. This fosters a sense of ownership and participation among members.

How DAOs Differ from Traditional Organizations

DAOs represent a significant departure from traditional organizational structures. Here are some key differences:

- **No Central Authority:** Traditional organizations often have a hierarchical structure with a central authority making decisions. DAOs, on the other hand, are governed by their members, with decisions made through voting or other consensus mechanisms. This eliminates the need for a central authority and promotes a more democratic and participatory approach to governance.
- **Transparency and Immutability:** In traditional organizations, decisions and actions might be obscured or subject to manipulation. In DAOs, all actions are recorded on the blockchain, making them transparent and immutable. This ensures that all decisions and actions are

publicly visible and cannot be altered or deleted, fostering trust and accountability.
- **Automation and Efficiency:** DAOs can automate many processes through smart contracts, reducing bureaucracy and increasing efficiency. This can streamline operations, reduce costs, and improve the speed of decision-making.
- **Global Reach:** DAOs can have members from all over the world, transcending geographical boundaries and enabling global collaboration. This opens up new possibilities for organizing and coordinating activities on a global scale.

Real-World Examples of DAOs

- **MakerDAO:** MakerDAO is a decentralized organization that governs the DAI stablecoin. It allows users to borrow DAI against collateralized assets and participate in the governance of the DAI ecosystem.
- **Uniswap:** Uniswap is a decentralized exchange (DEX) that is governed by a DAO. UNI token holders can vote on proposals related to the development and operation of the exchange.
- **Compound Finance:** Compound Finance is a decentralized lending and borrowing platform that is also governed by a DAO. COMP token holders can vote on proposals related to interest rates, collateralization ratios, and other parameters of the platform.
- **Gitcoin:** Gitcoin is a platform that uses a DAO to fund and support open-source projects. Contributors can earn rewards for completing tasks and contributing to projects, and the community votes on which projects receive funding.

Exercise:

Research some other DAOs and explore their governance structures and voting mechanisms. How do they make decisions?

How are funds managed? How can members participate in the governance process?

By understanding the concepts and characteristics of DAOs, you're gaining insights into a new paradigm of organizational structure and governance. DAOs offer a powerful way to create decentralized, transparent, and community-driven organizations that can operate efficiently and effectively in the digital age.

9.2 Building a Basic DAO

This is where you'll put your Solidity skills to the test and create a simple decentralized autonomous organization that can manage funds and make decisions collectively. Think of it like constructing the foundation of a new community, where members can contribute, propose ideas, and vote on how to allocate resources.

Core Components of a Basic DAO

A basic DAO typically includes the following components:

- **Treasury:** A wallet address that holds the DAO's funds. This is where members contribute funds and where funds are disbursed based on proposals that pass.
- **Membership:** A way to track who is a member of the DAO. This could be a simple list of addresses or a more sophisticated system involving tokens or NFTs.
- **Proposal Mechanism:** A way for members to create proposals for how the DAO should use its funds or make decisions.
- **Voting Mechanism:** A way for members to vote on proposals. This could be a simple majority vote or a more complex system involving weighted voting or quadratic voting.
- **Execution:** A mechanism for executing proposals that have passed the voting process.

Example Code: A Simple DAO Contract

Solidity

```solidity
pragma solidity ^0.8.0;

contract BasicDAO {

    // Address of the DAO's treasury

    address payable public treasury;

    // Mapping to store member contributions

    mapping(address => uint256) public contributions;

    // Array to store proposals

    Proposal[] public proposals;

    // Struct to represent a proposal

    struct Proposal {

        string description;

        address payable recipient;

        uint256 amount;

        uint256 yesVotes;

        uint256 noVotes;

        bool executed;

    }

    // Constructor to initialize the treasury
```

```solidity
    constructor() {

        treasury = payable(msg.sender); // Make the deployer the initial treasury controller

    }

    // Function to contribute to the DAO

    function contribute() public payable {

        contributions[msg.sender] += msg.value;

    }

    // Function to create a proposal

    function createProposal(string memory description, address payable recipient, uint256 amount) public {

        require(contributions[msg.sender] > 0, "You must contribute to create a proposal.");

        proposals.push(Proposal({

            description: description,

            recipient: recipient,

            amount: amount,

            yesVotes: 0,

            noVotes: 0,

            executed: false

        }));
```

```solidity
    }

    // Function to vote on a proposal
    function voteOnProposal(uint256 proposalId, bool vote) public {
        require(contributions[msg.sender] > 0, "You must contribute to vote.");
        Proposal storage proposal = proposals[proposalId];
        require(!proposal.executed, "Proposal already executed.");
        if (vote) {
            proposal.yesVotes += contributions[msg.sender];
        } else {
            proposal.noVotes += contributions[msg.sender];
        }
    }

    // Function to execute a proposal
    function executeProposal(uint256 proposalId) public {
        Proposal storage proposal = proposals[proposalId];
```

```
        require(!proposal.executed, "Proposal
already executed.");

        require(proposal.yesVotes >
proposal.noVotes, "Proposal failed.");

        proposal.executed = true;


proposal.recipient.transfer(proposal.amount);

    }

}
```

Explanation:

- This contract defines a BasicDAO with a treasury address to hold funds and a contributions mapping to track member contributions.
- The contribute function allows members to contribute Ether to the DAO.
- The createProposal function allows members who have contributed to create proposals. Each proposal includes a description, a recipient address, and an amount of Ether to be sent.
- The voteOnProposal function allows members to vote on proposals. The weight of their vote is proportional to their contribution.
- The executeProposal function allows anyone to execute a proposal if it has passed the voting process (more yes votes than no votes).

Key Improvements:

- **Proposal Struct:** We've introduced a Proposal struct to organize the data associated with each proposal.

- **Contribution Requirement:** Members must contribute to the DAO before they can create or vote on proposals.
- **Vote Weighting:** Votes are weighted based on the member's contribution.
- **Execution Logic:** The executeProposal function includes checks to prevent a proposal from being executed multiple times.

Real-World Examples:

Many DAOs in the real world use similar structures and functionalities to manage their operations:

- **MakerDAO:** MakerDAO uses a complex system of smart contracts and governance tokens (MKR) to manage the DAI stablecoin.
- **Compound Finance:** Compound Finance uses a DAO to govern its lending and borrowing platform, allowing COMP token holders to vote on proposals related to interest rates and other parameters.
- **Decentralized Autonomous Organizations (DAOs):** DAOs are organizations governed by code and run by communities, allowing for decentralized decision-making and governance.

Exercise:

Try modifying the BasicDAO contract to:

- Add a minimum contribution requirement for creating proposals.
- Implement a time limit for voting on proposals.
- Allow members to withdraw their contributions.
- Add a function to change the DAO's treasury address.

By building this basic DAO, you're gaining a practical understanding of how DAOs can be implemented using Solidity. This foundation will allow you to explore more complex DAO structures and governance mechanisms as you continue your Web3 development journey.

9.3 Governance and Voting Mechanisms

Let's talk about how decisions are made in a DAO! This is where the "autonomous" part of the Decentralized Autonomous Organization really comes into play. Since there's no central authority calling the shots, DAOs rely on governance and voting mechanisms to make collective decisions in a fair and transparent manner. Think of it like a democracy, where citizens (DAO members) have a say in how their community is run.

Why is Governance Important for DAOs?

Governance is crucial for DAOs because it provides a framework for:

- **Making Decisions:** DAOs need a way to make decisions about how to use their funds, allocate resources, and set the direction of the organization.
- **Resolving Disputes:** A clear governance process helps resolve disputes and disagreements among members.
- **Adapting to Change:** DAOs need to be able to adapt to changing circumstances and make decisions about how to evolve and improve over time.
- **Ensuring Fairness:** A well-designed governance system ensures that all members have a fair say in the decision-making process.

Voting Mechanisms

There are various voting mechanisms that DAOs can use, each with its own advantages and disadvantages. Let's explore some of the most common ones:

1. Token-Based Voting

This is the most common voting mechanism in DAOs. Members who hold governance tokens can vote on proposals. The weight of their vote is often proportional to the number of tokens they hold. This is similar to how shareholders in a company have voting rights proportional to their shares.

Pros:

- Simple and easy to understand.
- Aligns incentives, as token holders have a vested interest in the success of the DAO.

Cons:

- Can lead to concentration of power if a small number of members hold a large proportion of the tokens.
- Might not accurately reflect the diversity of opinions within the DAO.

Example:

In MakerDAO, MKR token holders can vote on proposals related to the DAI stablecoin, such as adjusting interest rates or adding new collateral types.

2. Quadratic Voting

Quadratic voting is a more complex voting mechanism that aims to give more weight to smaller stakeholders. It uses a quadratic formula to calculate voting power, where the cost of each vote increases quadratically with the number of votes cast. This means that it becomes increasingly expensive to cast more votes, encouraging voters to spread their votes across multiple proposals.

Pros:

- Gives more power to smaller stakeholders, promoting a more balanced decision-making process.
- Encourages thoughtful voting and discourages vote manipulation.

Cons:

- Can be more complex to implement and understand.
- Might not be suitable for all types of decisions.

Example:

Gitcoin Grants uses quadratic voting to allocate funding to open-source projects. This allows smaller donors to have a greater impact on the funding decisions.

3. Delegated Voting

In delegated voting, members can delegate their voting power to other members who they trust to represent their interests. This can be useful for DAOs with a large number of members, as it allows for more efficient decision-making without requiring every member to participate in every vote.

Pros:

- Improves efficiency by allowing knowledgeable or dedicated members to make decisions on behalf of others.
- Reduces the burden on individual members to participate in every vote.

Cons:

- Can lead to centralization of power if a small number of delegates hold a large amount of voting power.
- Requires trust in the delegates to represent the interests of the delegators.

Example:

Some DAOs use delegated voting to elect a council or board of directors who are responsible for making key decisions.

4. Conviction Voting

Conviction voting allows members to signal their conviction for a proposal over time. The longer a member supports a proposal, the more weight their vote carries. This mechanism favors proposals with sustained support and discourages short-term or impulsive voting.

Pros:

- Favors proposals with long-term support and discourages short-term thinking.
- Can be more resistant to vote manipulation.

Cons:

- Can be slow to reach decisions, as it requires time for conviction to accumulate.
- Might not be suitable for all types of decisions.

Example:

Some DAOs use conviction voting to make decisions about long-term strategy or funding allocation.

Implementing Voting Mechanisms in Solidity

You can implement these voting mechanisms in your Solidity contracts using various techniques:

- **Token balances:** Use token balances to determine voting power.
- **Data structures:** Use data structures like mappings and arrays to track votes and calculate results.

- **Modifiers:** Use modifiers to restrict voting to eligible members or enforce voting rules.

Exercise:

Try modifying the BasicDAO contract from the previous section to implement a different voting mechanism, such as quadratic voting or delegated voting.

By understanding and implementing different governance and voting mechanisms, you can create DAOs that are truly decentralized, democratic, and responsive to the needs of their communities. This is a crucial aspect of building successful and sustainable DAOs that can achieve their goals and make a positive impact in the world.

9.4 DAO Security Considerations

In the world of DAOs, where code is law and funds are often managed autonomously, security is absolutely paramount. Think of it like building a fortress to protect your community's treasury and ensure that the DAO operates as intended. Any vulnerability or weakness in your DAO's design or implementation can have serious consequences, potentially leading to financial loss, governance attacks, or even the complete collapse of the organization.

Why is DAO Security So Important?

DAOs often manage significant amounts of funds and make important decisions that affect their members. A security breach could lead to:

- **Loss of Funds:** Attackers could exploit vulnerabilities to steal funds from the DAO's treasury.
- **Governance Attacks:** Malicious actors could manipulate the voting process to gain control of the DAO or pass

proposals that benefit themselves at the expense of other members.
- **Reputation Damage:** A security incident could damage the reputation of the DAO, leading to a loss of trust and participation from members.

Key Security Considerations for DAOs

Here are some crucial security considerations to keep in mind when designing and building your DAO:

1. Smart Contract Vulnerabilities

The foundation of any DAO's security lies in the security of its smart contracts. These contracts govern the DAO's operations, manage its funds, and enforce its rules. Any vulnerability in these contracts can be exploited by attackers.

Here are some common smart contract vulnerabilities to watch out for:

- **Reentrancy:** As we discussed in Chapter 5, reentrancy attacks can allow an attacker to repeatedly execute a function, potentially draining funds from the DAO's treasury.
- **Integer Overflows and Underflows:** These vulnerabilities can lead to unexpected behavior in your contracts, potentially allowing attackers to manipulate balances or bypass security checks.
- **Logic Errors:** Flaws in the contract's logic can allow attackers to exploit unintended behavior or gain unauthorized access to funds or functionalities.
- **Access Control Issues:** Make sure that only authorized users or contracts can access sensitive functions or data within your DAO's contracts.

Mitigation Strategies:

- **Thorough Testing:** Write comprehensive tests to cover various scenarios and edge cases.
- **Professional Audits:** Have your contracts audited by experienced security professionals to identify potential vulnerabilities.
- **Use Secure Libraries:** Use well-tested and audited libraries like OpenZeppelin to implement common functionalities securely.
- **Follow Security Best Practices:** Adhere to secure coding practices and design principles to minimize the risk of vulnerabilities.

2. Governance Attacks

Governance attacks target the DAO's decision-making process, aiming to manipulate votes or gain control of the DAO. These attacks can take various forms:

- **Sybil Attacks:** An attacker creates multiple fake accounts to gain a disproportionate amount of voting power.
- **Vote Buying:** An attacker bribes members to vote in their favor.
- **Flash Loan Attacks:** An attacker uses flash loans (borrowing and repaying a large amount of cryptocurrency within a single transaction) to manipulate token prices and influence voting outcomes.

Mitigation Strategies:

- **Identity Verification:** Implement mechanisms to verify the identity of members to prevent Sybil attacks.
- **Quadratic Voting:** Use quadratic voting to give more weight to smaller stakeholders and reduce the impact of large token holders.

- **Time-Locked Voting:** Introduce time delays in the voting process to give members time to analyze proposals and detect potential manipulation.
- **Community Awareness:** Educate DAO members about potential governance attacks and encourage them to participate actively in the governance process.

3. Oracle Manipulation

Many DAOs rely on external data from oracles to make decisions or trigger actions. Oracles are sources of information that provide data from the real world to the blockchain. However, if these oracles are compromised or manipulated, it can lead to incorrect decisions or unintended consequences within the DAO.

Mitigation Strategies:

- **Use Decentralized Oracles:** Use decentralized oracle networks like Chainlink, which provide reliable and tamper-proof data feeds from multiple sources.
- **Data Validation:** Implement mechanisms to validate data from oracles before using it in your contracts.
- **Redundancy:** Use multiple oracles to reduce reliance on a single source of data.

4. Key Management

The private keys that control the DAO's treasury and other critical functions are valuable targets for attackers. If these keys are compromised, attackers could gain control of the DAO's funds or manipulate its operations.

Mitigation Strategies:

- **Multi-signature Wallets:** Use multi-signature wallets that require multiple parties to authorize transactions, making it more difficult for attackers to steal funds.

- **Hardware Wallets:** Store private keys on secure hardware wallets that are offline and protected from online attacks.
- **Time-Locked Wallets:** Use time-locked wallets that restrict access to funds for a certain period, giving time to detect and respond to potential attacks.

Real-world examples:

- **The DAO Hack:** The infamous DAO hack in 2016 exploited a reentrancy vulnerability in a DAO contract, resulting in the loss of millions of dollars worth of Ether.
- **Parity Wallet Hacks:** Several vulnerabilities in Parity multi-signature wallets led to significant losses in 2017, highlighting the importance of secure key management.

Exercise:

Research some recent security incidents involving DAOs. What vulnerabilities were exploited? How could these incidents have been prevented?

By understanding and addressing these security considerations, you can build DAOs that are resilient to attacks and protect the interests of their members. Security is an ongoing process that requires constant vigilance and adaptation to new threats and vulnerabilities. By prioritizing security in your DAO design and implementation, you can create a trustworthy and sustainable organization that can thrive in the decentralized world.

Chapter 10: Interacting with Other Blockchains

Think of it like exploring different countries – each country has its own culture, language, and way of doing things. Similarly, each blockchain has its own ecosystem, technologies, and use cases. In this chapter, we'll learn how to interact with other blockchains, expanding the possibilities for your dApps and connecting to a wider world of decentralized innovation.

10.1 Cross-chain Communication

In the Web3 space, cross-chain communication enables interoperability between different blockchains. This means that different blockchains can talk to each other, exchange data, and transfer assets seamlessly. This opens up a whole new world of possibilities for decentralized applications, allowing them to leverage the strengths of different blockchains and create more complex and interconnected systems.

Why is Cross-chain Communication Important?

Here are some key reasons why cross-chain communication is essential for the future of Web3:

- **Interoperability:** It allows different blockchains to work together, breaking down silos and fostering a more interconnected and collaborative ecosystem. This is crucial for the growth and adoption of blockchain technology, as it allows users to seamlessly move assets and data between different platforms.
- **Scalability:** Cross-chain communication can help improve scalability by distributing transactions and data across multiple blockchains. This can reduce congestion on individual chains and improve overall network performance.

- **Specialization:** Different blockchains might specialize in different functionalities or use cases. Cross-chain communication allows developers to leverage the strengths of each chain and build applications that combine the best of different worlds.
- **User Experience:** Cross-chain communication can improve the user experience by making it easier to move assets and interact with dApps across different chains. This can reduce friction and make blockchain technology more accessible to a wider audience.

Challenges of Cross-chain Communication

Building bridges between blockchains is no easy feat. There are several challenges that developers need to overcome:

- **Different Architectures:** Each blockchain has its own unique architecture, consensus mechanism, and security model. This makes it challenging to create a universal communication protocol that works seamlessly across all chains. It's like trying to build a bridge between two countries with different terrain, climates, and engineering standards.
- **Security Risks:** Cross-chain communication can introduce security risks, as it involves transferring assets and data between different trust environments. It's like ensuring that goods and people can safely cross a border without any security breaches.
- **Scalability:** Handling a large volume of cross-chain transactions can be challenging, as it requires coordination and consensus between different blockchains. It's like ensuring that a bridge can handle heavy traffic flow without collapsing.

Approaches to Cross-chain Communication

Despite these challenges, developers are actively working on various approaches to enable cross-chain communication. Here are some of the most promising solutions:

- **Bridges:** Bridges are specialized protocols that connect two or more blockchains, allowing for the transfer of assets and data between them. They act like intermediaries that facilitate communication and ensure compatibility between different chains. Think of them as the customs and immigration offices at a border crossing, ensuring that goods and people can move between countries smoothly and securely.
- **Interoperability Protocols:** These protocols aim to create a standardized framework for cross-chain communication, enabling seamless interaction between different blockchains. They're like establishing international trade agreements that define common rules and standards for commerce between countries.
- **Sidechains:** Sidechains are separate blockchains that are interoperable with a main chain, allowing for the transfer of assets and data between them. They're like building a smaller, specialized road that connects to the main highway, allowing for more efficient traffic flow for specific types of vehicles.

Real-world examples:

- **Wormhole:** Wormhole is a popular bridge that connects various blockchains, including Ethereum, Solana, Terra, and Binance Smart Chain. It allows users to transfer tokens and other assets between these chains.
- **Cosmos:** Cosmos is an ecosystem of interoperable blockchains that uses the Inter-Blockchain Communication (IBC) protocol for cross-chain communication. This allows

different blockchains within the Cosmos ecosystem to communicate and exchange data with each other.
- **Polkadot:** Polkadot is another platform that aims to enable interoperability between different blockchains. It uses a "relay chain" to connect different "parachains," allowing them to share information and transfer assets.

Exercise:

Research some popular blockchain bridges and explore their functionalities. How do they work? What chains do they connect? What types of assets can be transferred?

By understanding cross-chain communication, you're gaining insights into one of the most important frontiers in blockchain technology. It's a complex but rapidly evolving field that has the potential to unlock the true power of Web3, creating a more interconnected and interoperable ecosystem of decentralized applications and services.

10.2 Web3 Libraries and APIs

These are essential tools for any Web3 developer, providing the building blocks for interacting with different blockchains and building decentralized applications. Think of them as your trusty companions on your Web3 journey, providing you with the tools and guidance you need to navigate this exciting landscape.

What are Web3 Libraries and APIs?

A Web3 library is a collection of code that provides functions and tools for interacting with a blockchain. It acts as an intermediary between your application and the blockchain, handling the complexities of communication and data formatting.

An API (Application Programming Interface) is a set of rules and specifications that allow different software systems to communicate with each other. In the context of Web3, APIs provide a way for your application to access data and functionality from a blockchain.

Why Use Web3 Libraries and APIs?

- **Simplified Interaction:** They abstract away the complexities of blockchain interactions, making it easier for developers to build dApps. You don't need to be a blockchain expert to start building!
- **Standardization:** They provide a standardized way to interact with different blockchains, reducing the learning curve and making it easier to switch between different platforms. It's like having a universal remote control that can work with different TV brands.
- **Increased Efficiency:** They handle many of the low-level details of blockchain interaction, allowing you to focus on building the core logic of your dApp. This can save you a lot of time and effort.
- **Community Support:** Most popular Web3 libraries have large and active communities, providing support, documentation, and resources to help you along the way.

Popular Web3 Libraries

Here are some of the most popular Web3 libraries used by developers:

- **Web3.js:** This is the most widely used JavaScript library for interacting with Ethereum and other EVM-compatible blockchains. It provides a comprehensive set of functions for managing accounts, sending transactions, interacting with smart contracts, and more.
- **Ethers.js:** Another popular JavaScript library for Ethereum development. It's known for its clean API,

improved security features, and smaller size compared to Web3.js.
- **Web3.py:** If you prefer Python, Web3.py is a great choice. It provides similar functionalities to Web3.js but in a Pythonic way.
- **ethers-rs:** For Rust developers, ethers-rs offers a comprehensive and efficient way to interact with Ethereum and other EVM-compatible chains.

Key Functionalities of Web3 Libraries

Most Web3 libraries provide the following core functionalities:

- **Connecting to a Blockchain:** Establish a connection to a specific blockchain network, such as the Ethereum mainnet or a testnet. This usually involves specifying a node provider (like Infura or Alchemy) or running your own node.
- **Managing Accounts:** Create and manage accounts, generate private keys, sign transactions, and interact with wallets like MetaMask.
- **Interacting with Smart Contracts:** Call functions on smart contracts, read data from contracts, and send transactions to contracts. This involves encoding function calls and decoding return values.
- **Sending Transactions:** Send various types of transactions, such as Ether transfers, token transfers, or contract deployments. This includes estimating gas costs, setting gas prices, and handling transaction confirmations.
- **Estimating Gas Costs:** Estimate the gas cost of a transaction before sending it. This helps users understand the cost of interacting with your dApp and prevents transactions from failing due to insufficient gas.
- **Accessing Blockchain Data:** Retrieve various types of data from the blockchain, such as block information, transaction history, and account balances.

Example Code: Using Web3.js to Interact with a Contract

JavaScript

```javascript
// Import the Web3.js library

const Web3 = require('web3');

// Connect to an Ethereum node provider (e.g., Infura)

const web3 = new Web3('https://mainnet.infura.io/v3/YOUR_INFURA_PROJECT_ID');

// Define the contract ABI (Application Binary Interface) and address

const contractABI = [...]; // Your contract's ABI

const contractAddress = '0x...'; // Your contract's address

// Create a contract instance

const myContract = new web3.eth.Contract(contractABI, contractAddress);

// Call a function on the contract

myContract.methods.myFunction().call()
  .then(result => {
    console.log("Result:", result);
  })
  .catch(error => {
```

```
    console.error("Error:", error);
});
```

This example shows how to use Web3.js to connect to an Ethereum node, create a contract instance, and call a function on the contract.

Real-World Examples

- **MetaMask:** MetaMask, a popular browser extension wallet, uses Web3.js to interact with the Ethereum blockchain and enable users to manage their accounts and interact with dApps.
- **Uniswap Interface:** The Uniswap decentralized exchange uses Web3.js to connect to the Ethereum blockchain and allow users to trade tokens.
- **NFT Marketplaces:** NFT marketplaces like OpenSea use Web3 libraries to facilitate the creation, buying, and selling of NFTs.

Exercise:

1. Choose a Web3 library (Web3.js, Ethers.js, or Web3.py) and install it in your development environment.
2. Explore the library's documentation and try out some of its basic functions, such as connecting to a testnet and retrieving account information.
3. Find a simple smart contract example and use the library to interact with its functions.

By understanding and using Web3 libraries and APIs, you're gaining essential tools for building decentralized applications. They simplify the process of interacting with blockchains, allowing you to focus on creating innovative and impactful dApps that can transform the way we interact and transact online.

10.3 Exploring Other EVM-Compatible Chains

Think of it like exploring different cities within the same country. Each city has its own character, attractions, and way of life, but they all share a common language and culture. Similarly, many blockchains are EVM-compatible, meaning they can execute Solidity code and support Ethereum-like dApps, but they might offer different benefits like lower fees, faster transactions, or specialized functionalities.

Why Explore Other EVM-Compatible Chains?

Here are some compelling reasons to venture beyond the Ethereum mainnet:

- **Lower Fees:** One of the main challenges with Ethereum is the high gas fees associated with transactions. Some EVM-compatible chains offer significantly lower transaction fees, making them more attractive for users and developers. This can be especially important for applications that involve frequent or small transactions.
- **Faster Transactions:** Some chains have faster block times and transaction confirmation speeds than Ethereum. This can lead to a more responsive and efficient user experience, especially for time-sensitive applications like gaming or decentralized exchanges.
- **Scalability:** Ethereum has faced scalability challenges, leading to network congestion and high gas fees during periods of high activity. Some EVM-compatible chains offer better scalability solutions, allowing for a higher throughput of transactions and a smoother user experience.
- **Specialized Functionalities:** Some chains offer specialized functionalities or features that might be beneficial for specific use cases. For example, some chains

focus on privacy, while others might offer enhanced support for specific types of dApps or tokens.
- **Community and Ecosystem:** Each blockchain has its own unique community and ecosystem of developers, projects, and users. Exploring other chains can expose you to new ideas, collaborations, and opportunities.

Popular EVM-Compatible Chains

Let's take a look at some of the most popular EVM-compatible chains:

- **Polygon:** Polygon is a layer-2 scaling solution for Ethereum that offers faster and cheaper transactions. It's like building a high-speed expressway on top of the existing road network to alleviate traffic congestion. Polygon has become a popular choice for many dApps and projects that want to benefit from Ethereum's security and ecosystem while enjoying lower fees and faster transactions.
- **Binance Smart Chain (BSC):** BSC is a blockchain developed by Binance, one of the largest cryptocurrency exchanges. It offers high throughput and low fees, making it attractive for DeFi applications and other high-volume use cases.
- **Avalanche:** Avalanche is a high-performance blockchain platform that supports smart contracts and dApps. It uses a unique consensus mechanism that allows for fast transaction speeds and high throughput.
- **Fantom:** Fantom is another fast and scalable blockchain platform with low transaction fees. It's known for its focus on DeFi and its growing ecosystem of dApps.
- **Arbitrum and Optimism:** These are layer-2 scaling solutions that aim to improve Ethereum's scalability and reduce transaction costs. They use optimistic rollup technology, which bundles transactions off-chain and

submits them to the Ethereum mainnet in batches, reducing the overall gas costs.

How to Interact with EVM-Compatible Chains

Interacting with EVM-compatible chains is similar to interacting with Ethereum. You can use familiar tools and libraries like MetaMask, Web3.js, and Remix. However, you'll need to configure them to connect to the specific chain you want to use.

Here are some general steps:

1. **Choose a Chain:** Select the EVM-compatible chain you want to interact with.
2. **Configure Your Tools:** Configure your development environment (e.g., Remix) or Web3 library (e.g., Web3.js) to connect to the chosen chain's network. This usually involves specifying the chain's RPC URL (Remote Procedure Call URL), which provides access to a node on that network.
3. **Deploy and Interact:** Deploy your contracts and interact with them using the same techniques you would use on Ethereum.

Real-world examples:

- **Aave on Polygon:** The Aave lending and borrowing protocol is deployed on Polygon to offer users faster and cheaper transactions. This allows users to borrow and lend cryptocurrencies with lower fees and faster confirmation times.
- **Curve Finance on Fantom:** Curve Finance, a popular decentralized exchange for stablecoins, is also deployed on Fantom to provide users with a more efficient and cost-effective trading experience.
- **SushiSwap on Multiple Chains:** SushiSwap, another popular DEX, is deployed on multiple chains, including

Ethereum, Polygon, and Avalanche, allowing users to trade tokens across different platforms.

Exercise:

1. Choose an EVM-compatible chain that interests you.
2. Configure your Remix environment to connect to that chain's network.
3. Deploy the SimpleStorage contract from Chapter 2 to that chain and interact with its functions.
4. Compare the gas costs and transaction speeds with deploying and interacting with the same contract on the Ethereum mainnet.

By exploring other EVM-compatible chains, you can expand the possibilities for your dApps and tap into a wider range of blockchain technologies and communities. This allows you to choose the best platform for your specific needs and leverage the strengths of different blockchains to create innovative and impactful decentralized applications.

Chapter 11: The Future of Solidity and Web3

Congratulations on making it this far! You've journeyed through the core concepts of Solidity, built your own smart contracts, and explored the exciting world of decentralized applications. But the Web3 landscape is constantly evolving, with new technologies and trends emerging all the time. In this final chapter, we'll look ahead to the future of Solidity and Web3, exploring the emerging trends that are shaping this space and the exciting possibilities that lie ahead.

11.1 Emerging Trends and Technologies

In this section, we'll explore some of the most promising trends that are shaping the future of Solidity and Web3 development. These trends are not just fleeting fads – they represent fundamental shifts in how we think about blockchain technology, decentralized applications, and the future of the internet.

1. Layer-2 Scaling Solutions:

As we discussed in previous chapters, Ethereum has faced scalability challenges. The increasing popularity of dApps and NFTs has led to network congestion and high gas fees, making it expensive and sometimes slow to use.

Layer-2 scaling solutions aim to address these challenges by moving transactions off the main Ethereum blockchain (Layer-1) to secondary chains or protocols (Layer-2). This is like building express lanes on a highway to alleviate traffic congestion. By processing transactions off the main chain, Layer-2 solutions can significantly increase transaction throughput and reduce gas fees, making Ethereum more scalable and efficient.

Here are some popular types of Layer-2 solutions:

- **Rollups:** Rollups bundle multiple transactions together off-chain and submit them to the mainnet as a single transaction. This reduces the amount of data that needs to be processed on the main chain, resulting in lower gas costs and increased throughput. There are two main types of rollups:
    - **Optimistic Rollups:** These assume that transactions are valid unless challenged, providing fast transaction speeds but with a slight delay for finality. Examples include Optimism and Arbitrum.
    - **Zk-Rollups:** These use zero-knowledge proofs to verify the validity of transactions off-chain, providing high security and scalability. Examples include zkSync and StarkNet.
- **Sidechains:** Sidechains are separate blockchains that are interoperable with Ethereum. They can process transactions independently and then communicate with the mainnet to settle final results. This allows for greater flexibility and scalability, as sidechains can have their own consensus mechanisms and token economics. Polygon is a popular example of a sidechain.
- **State Channels:** State channels allow participants to conduct multiple transactions off-chain and then settle the final state on the mainnet. This is particularly useful for applications that require frequent interactions, such as gaming or micropayments. It's like having a separate tab at a bar where you can run up a tab and then settle the final bill at the end of the night.

2. Improved Developer Tools

The Solidity development ecosystem is constantly improving, with new tools and frameworks emerging to make it easier to build, test, and deploy smart contracts. These tools are like the power tools and specialized equipment that help construction workers build better and faster.

Some notable examples include:

- **Hardhat:** A development environment that provides a fast and flexible testing framework, debugging tools, and deployment scripts. It's like a comprehensive toolkit for Solidity developers, providing everything you need to build, test, and deploy your contracts efficiently.
- **Foundry:** A blazingly fast testing framework written in Rust that focuses on efficiency and developer experience. It's known for its speed and simplicity, making it a popular choice for developers who want to write tests quickly and easily.
- **Slither:** A static analysis tool that can identify potential vulnerabilities in your Solidity code. It's like a code inspector that checks your code for common security flaws and helps you fix them before they can be exploited.

These are just a few examples of the many tools and frameworks that are being developed to improve the Solidity development experience. As the ecosystem continues to mature, we can expect even more powerful and user-friendly tools to emerge, making it easier for developers to create secure and efficient dApps.

3. Cross-chain Interoperability

As we discussed in Chapter 10, cross-chain interoperability is becoming increasingly important in the Web3 space. New bridges and protocols are being developed to connect different blockchains, allowing for the seamless transfer of assets and data between them. This is like building bridges and tunnels to connect different cities and countries, enabling smoother transportation and communication.

This trend is leading to a more interconnected and collaborative blockchain ecosystem, where users can interact with dApps across different chains and developers can leverage the strengths of different platforms. It's like creating a global network of interconnected cities, each with its own unique character and offerings, but all working together to create a richer and more vibrant world.

4. Decentralized Identity

Decentralized identity solutions are gaining traction, giving users more control over their digital identities and enabling secure and verifiable authentication. This is like having a digital passport that you control, allowing you to prove your identity without relying on centralized authorities or intermediaries.

This can reduce reliance on centralized identity providers, which are often vulnerable to data breaches and privacy violations. It also empowers users to manage their own online identities and choose how their personal information is used and shared.

5. Privacy-Enhancing Technologies

Privacy is a growing concern in the blockchain space, as many blockchains are transparent by design. New technologies like zero-knowledge proofs (ZKPs) and secure multi-party computation (MPC) are being used to enhance privacy in dApps and protect user data.

ZKPs allow you to prove that you know something without revealing the information itself. For example, you could prove that you are over 18 without revealing your exact age. MPC allows multiple parties to jointly compute a function without revealing their individual inputs. This can be used for privacy-preserving data sharing and analysis.

6. The Metaverse and Web3 Gaming:

The metaverse is a concept of a persistent, shared virtual world where users can interact with each other, participate in experiences, and own digital assets. It's like a virtual reality internet where you can work, play, socialize, and create.

NFTs and blockchain technology are playing a key role in the development of metaverses, enabling the creation of unique and valuable in-world assets and experiences. For example, you could own a virtual piece of land, a digital artwork, or a unique in-game item that is represented by an NFT.

Web3 gaming is also on the rise, with blockchain-based games offering players true ownership of in-game assets and new forms of gameplay and monetization. This can create more immersive and engaging gaming experiences, where players have a real stake in the game's economy and can contribute to its development.

7. Decentralized Governance:

DAOs are becoming increasingly popular for managing decentralized organizations and communities. New governance mechanisms and tools are being developed to improve the efficiency and security of DAO decision-making. This allows communities to make decisions collectively and transparently, without relying on central authorities.

8. The Rise of Alternative Blockchains:

While Ethereum remains the dominant platform for smart contracts, other blockchains are gaining traction, offering alternatives with different features and advantages. These include:

- **Solana:** A high-performance blockchain that boasts fast transaction speeds and low fees.

- **Polkadot:** A platform that aims to enable interoperability between different blockchains.
- **Cosmos:** An ecosystem of interoperable blockchains that focuses on scalability and sovereignty.

These alternative blockchains are expanding the Web3 ecosystem, providing developers with more choices and fostering innovation in different areas.

Real-world examples:

- **The Merge:** Ethereum's transition to a proof-of-stake consensus mechanism, known as "The Merge," significantly reduced its energy consumption and improved its scalability.
- **Layer-2 adoption:** Many dApps are migrating to Layer-2 solutions like Polygon and Arbitrum to reduce gas fees and improve transaction speeds.
- **Cross-chain bridges:** Bridges like Wormhole and Multichain are enabling the transfer of assets between different blockchains.

By staying informed about these emerging trends and technologies, you can position yourself at the forefront of Web3 innovation and contribute to the development of the decentralized future.

11.2 Solidity Development Roadmap

In this section, we'll take a peek into the Solidity development roadmap, exploring the key areas of focus and the exciting advancements that are on the horizon. This will give you a glimpse into the future of Solidity and help you stay ahead of the curve as a Web3 developer.

Key Focus Areas in Solidity Development

The Solidity development roadmap is guided by several key goals:

- **Improved Security:** Security is paramount in the world of smart contracts. The Solidity team is constantly working on improving the security of the language by adding new features, fixing bugs, and providing better tooling for security analysis. This is like reinforcing the walls of your smart contract fortress, making it more resistant to attacks and vulnerabilities.
- **Enhanced Performance:** Optimizing the compiler and runtime environment to improve the performance and efficiency of Solidity code is a continuous effort. This involves making the code execute faster, use less gas, and consume fewer resources. It's like fine-tuning the engine of a car to make it more fuel-efficient and powerful.
- **Increased Developer Experience:** Making the language easier to learn and use is a priority. This involves providing better error messages, improving documentation, and creating more user-friendly tools. It's like making the tools and equipment in your workshop more ergonomic and intuitive, so you can focus on building and creating.
- **New Features:** The Solidity team is always exploring new features to add to the language, supporting more complex and sophisticated smart contract development. This could include new data types, control flow structures, or libraries that make it easier to express complex logic and build advanced dApps. It's like adding new tools and materials to your workshop, expanding your creative possibilities.

Specific Improvements and Features

Here are some specific improvements and features that are being worked on or have been recently introduced in Solidity:

- **Yul Optimizer:** Yul is an intermediate language that Solidity code is compiled into before being converted to bytecode. The Yul optimizer is a powerful tool that can

significantly improve the gas efficiency of your contracts by optimizing the Yul code.
- **Error Handling Improvements:** Solidity is introducing new error handling mechanisms to make it easier to handle errors and provide more informative error messages. This can help developers write more robust and user-friendly contracts.
- **User-Defined Value Types:** Solidity is adding support for user-defined value types, which allow developers to define their own custom data types with specific properties and behaviors. This can improve code readability and organization.
- **Immutable Variables:** Immutable variables are variables that can only be set once during contract creation. This can improve the security and efficiency of your contracts by preventing accidental or malicious modification of critical data.
- **Enhanced Debugging Tools:** The Solidity team is working on improving the debugging tools available to developers, making it easier to identify and fix errors in their code.

Staying Updated with Solidity Development

The best way to stay up-to-date with the latest developments in Solidity is to follow the official resources:

- Solidity Documentation: The official Solidity documentation is a comprehensive resource that provides detailed information about the language, its features, and its development roadmap.
- Solidity Blog: The Solidity blog provides updates on new releases, features, and events in the Solidity community.
- Solidity GitHub Repository: The Solidity GitHub repository is where the source code for the Solidity compiler is hosted.

You can follow the development progress, contribute to the project, and report issues.
- Solidity Community Forum: The Solidity community forum is a great place to connect with other developers, ask questions, and discuss the latest developments in the language.

Real-World Impact

These ongoing improvements in Solidity have a direct impact on the Web3 ecosystem:

- More Secure dApps: Enhanced security features and better tooling help developers create more secure dApps, protecting users' funds and data.
- Reduced Gas Costs: Gas optimization efforts make dApps more affordable to use, increasing accessibility and adoption.
- Improved Performance: Performance enhancements lead to faster and more responsive dApps, providing a better user experience.
- Increased Innovation: New features and capabilities in Solidity empower developers to create more innovative and sophisticated dApps, pushing the boundaries of what's possible with blockchain technology.

Exercise:

Explore the Solidity documentation and find information about a recent or upcoming feature that interests you. Try experimenting with this feature in a simple contract to understand how it works and how it can be used to improve your dApp development.

By staying informed about the Solidity development roadmap, you can ensure that you're using the latest and greatest features of the language and contributing to the advancement of the Web3 ecosystem. It's an exciting time to be a Solidity developer, as the language continues to evolve and empower the creation of innovative and impactful decentralized applications.

11.3 The Evolving Web3 Landscape

As you embark on your journey as a Web3 developer, it's essential to keep your finger on the pulse of this evolving landscape. New trends, technologies, and challenges are constantly shaping the future of this space. By staying informed and adaptable, you can ensure that your skills and knowledge remain relevant and that you can contribute to the exciting developments that lie ahead.

Key Trends Shaping the Future of Web3

Here are some of the key trends that are driving the evolution of the Web3 landscape:

1. **The Rise of Layer-2 Solutions**

As we discussed in the previous section, Ethereum's scalability challenges have led to the rise of Layer-2 scaling solutions. These solutions are becoming increasingly important for improving the efficiency and affordability of dApps. We can expect to see further development and adoption of Layer-2 technologies, such as Optimistic Rollups, Zk-Rollups, and sidechains, as the Web3 ecosystem continues to grow.

2. **Cross-Chain Interoperability**

The ability for different blockchains to communicate and interact with each other is becoming increasingly important. Cross-chain bridges and interoperability protocols are enabling the transfer of assets and data between different chains, fostering a more interconnected and collaborative ecosystem. We can expect to see more bridges and protocols emerge, connecting various blockchains and enabling new forms of cross-chain interaction.

3. **Decentralized Identity**

Decentralized identity solutions are gaining traction, giving users more control over their digital identities and enabling secure and verifiable authentication. This trend is driven by the growing concern over data privacy and the increasing number of data breaches on centralized platforms. We can expect to see more innovative solutions emerge, empowering users to manage their own digital identities and interact with dApps in a more secure and private manner.

4. **Privacy-Enhancing Technologies**

Privacy is a fundamental right, and it's becoming increasingly important in the Web3 space. New technologies like zero-knowledge proofs (ZKPs) and secure multi-party computation (MPC) are being used to enhance privacy in dApps and protect user data. We can expect to see wider adoption of these technologies as developers prioritize user privacy and build more privacy-preserving applications.

5. **The Metaverse and Web3 Gaming**

The metaverse is a concept of a persistent, shared virtual world where users can interact with each other, participate in experiences, and own digital assets. NFTs and blockchain technology are playing a key role in the development of metaverses, enabling the creation of unique and valuable in-world assets and experiences. We can expect to see significant growth in the metaverse space, with new virtual worlds and experiences emerging and attracting a growing user base.

Web3 gaming is also on the rise, with blockchain-based games offering players true ownership of in-game assets and new forms of gameplay and monetization. This trend is transforming the gaming industry, empowering players and creating new economic models for game developers. We can expect to see more innovative and immersive Web3 games emerge, pushing the boundaries of gaming and entertainment.

6. **Decentralized Governance**

Decentralized Autonomous Organizations (DAOs) are becoming increasingly popular for managing decentralized organizations and communities. New governance mechanisms and tools are being developed to improve the efficiency and security of DAO decision-making. We can expect to see more sophisticated DAO structures and governance models emerge, enabling more effective and inclusive community governance.

7. **The Rise of Alternative Blockchains**

While Ethereum remains the dominant platform for smart contracts, other blockchains are gaining traction, offering alternatives with different features and advantages. These include Solana, Polkadot, Cosmos, and others. Each of these blockchains has its own strengths and weaknesses, and we can expect to see a more diverse and competitive blockchain landscape in the future.

8. **Regulation and Compliance**

As the Web3 space matures, we can expect to see increased regulation and compliance requirements. This will bring both challenges and opportunities for developers, as they need to navigate the legal and regulatory landscape while building and deploying dApps.

9. **Increased Institutional Adoption**

Institutional interest in blockchain and Web3 is growing, with major companies and financial institutions exploring the potential of this technology. This could lead to increased investment and adoption of Web3 solutions, driving further innovation and growth in the space.

10. **Focus on Sustainability**

Sustainability is becoming an important consideration in the Web3 space, with concerns about the environmental impact of blockchain technology. We can expect to see more efforts to develop and adopt more energy-efficient consensus mechanisms and technologies.

Staying Ahead of the Curve

To stay informed about the evolving Web3 landscape, here are some resources you can follow:

- **Web3 News and Media:** Stay updated with the latest news and developments in the Web3 space by following reputable news sources and blogs.
- **Blockchain Conferences and Events:** Attend conferences and events to learn about the latest trends and connect with other developers and industry leaders.
- **Community Forums and Discussions:** Participate in online forums and discussions to engage with the Web3 community and stay informed about emerging trends and challenges.
- **Research Papers and Reports:** Read research papers and reports to gain deeper insights into specific technologies and trends.

The Future is Decentralized

The Web3 landscape is dynamic and full of possibilities. By staying informed, adaptable, and engaged, you can be a part of the exciting future of this technology and contribute to building a more decentralized, user-centric, and innovative internet.

Conclusion

Congratulations, aspiring Web3 developers! You've reached the end of our journey through the fascinating world of Solidity and smart contract development. We've covered a lot of ground, from the fundamental concepts of Web3 and the intricacies of the Solidity language to the complexities of designing, deploying, and interacting with smart contracts. You've even built your own tokens, NFTs, and a basic DAO! That's a remarkable achievement, and you should be proud of the progress you've made.

What You've Learned

Throughout this book, you've gained a solid understanding of:

- Web3 Fundamentals: You now grasp the core principles of Web3, including decentralization, blockchain technology, and the role of smart contracts in this new internet paradigm.
- Solidity Programming: You've mastered the essential elements of Solidity, from syntax and data types to functions, control flow, and object-oriented programming.
- Smart Contract Development: You've learned how to design, deploy, and interact with smart contracts, using tools like Remix, Hardhat, and Web3 libraries.
- Security Best Practices: You've explored common security vulnerabilities and learned how to write secure and robust smart contracts.
- Tokenization and NFTs: You've gained hands-on experience in creating ERC-20 tokens and ERC-721 NFTs, understanding their functionalities and potential applications.
- DAO Governance: You've learned how to build and interact with basic DAOs, exploring different governance and voting mechanisms.

- Beyond Ethereum: You've been introduced to other EVM-compatible chains and the broader Web3 landscape, expanding your knowledge and opportunities.

As you continue your Web3 development journey, remember that learning is an ongoing process. The Web3 space is constantly evolving, with new technologies and trends emerging all the time. Stay curious, keep learning, and never stop exploring the vast possibilities of this exciting field.

Here are some paths you can consider:

- Build Your Own dApps: Put your newfound skills to the test and build your own decentralized applications. Explore different use cases, experiment with new technologies, and contribute to the growing Web3 ecosystem.
- Contribute to Open-Source Projects: Join the vibrant community of open-source Web3 developers and contribute to projects that align with your interests.
- Deepen Your Expertise: Specialize in a particular area of Web3 development, such as DeFi, NFTs, DAOs, or security.
- Stay Informed: Keep up-to-date with the latest trends and technologies by following Web3 news sources, attending conferences, and participating in online communities.

Solidity has become the cornerstone of smart contract development on Ethereum and other EVM-compatible chains. Its versatility, efficiency, and growing ecosystem make it a powerful tool for building the decentralized future. As the language continues to evolve and improve, we can expect even more innovative and impactful applications to emerge.

Web3 is more than just a technological shift – it's a cultural and societal shift towards a more decentralized, user-centric, and transparent internet. By learning Solidity and contributing to the Web3 ecosystem, you're not only building exciting applications but also participating in a movement that has the potential to reshape the world.

Thank you for joining me on this journey through the world of Solidity and Web3 development. I hope this book has equipped you with the knowledge and skills you need to build a decentralized future and make a positive impact on the world. Happy coding!

www.ingramcontent.com/pod-product-compliance
Lightning Source LLC
Chambersburg PA
CBHW082247220526
45469CB00009B/2905